AUTHENTIC CHICAGO

THE FAIRWAY FLAPPER, THE LINCOLNWOOD LONE RANGER, THE WANDERING CHURCH — and — OTHER QUIRKY HISTORY

JOHN R. SCHMIDT

THE
History
PRESS

Published by The History Press
Charleston, SC
www.historypress.com

Copyright © 2023 by John R. Schmidt
All rights reserved

First published 2023

Manufactured in the United States

ISBN 9781467154918

Library of Congress Control Number: 2023938439

CONTENTS

CONTENTS

ACKNOWLEDGEMENTS

Most of my research was carried out at the Regenstein Library of the University of Chicago and at the Harold Washington Library in downtown Chicago. My thanks to the staffs at both places for their help. Thank you to Cheryl Ziegler, archivist at the Union League Club of Chicago, for digging through the archives to find the perfect photos for my needs. And thank you to Ben Gibson and Hilary Parrish of The History Press for guiding this book through to publication.

Thank you to my children, Nick Schmidt and Tracy Samantha Goodheart, for taking time out from their busy lives to provide feedback and suggestions. And last but most, thank you to my dear wife, Terri Schmidt, for her sharp insights, her encouragement, and her patience. Once again, I dedicate a book to Terri—not because I'm supposed to, but because she deserves it.

A.M.D.G.

INTRODUCTION

*A*uthentic Chicago is about the history most Chicagoans don't know—the *real* Chicago Way. It's an eclectic collection of short pieces that will raise a chuckle, or perhaps cause a groan, while flavored with a distinctive Chicago taste.

The book is about people. We meet the African American congressman who paved the way for Harold Washington and Barack Obama, the South Side Jewish girl who became the president of a South American country, the visiting Romanian queen who charmed the city, the misfit high school student who grew up to become Amelia Earhart.

The book is a city guide. It's about the forgotten landmarks that don't make it onto the typical tour route. It's about the Chicago version of "fly-over country"—interesting neighborhoods that most people drive by on their way to someplace else.

The book is about unusual stories. The airline that carried commuters between Northbrook and Midway, the ski resort on the city's Northwest Side, the church that crossed Ashland Avenue, the greatest train robbery in U.S. history.

And the book answers some timeless questions. Why does furniture sprout on Chicago streets after a blizzard? When were Chicagoans paid to smile? How do you make a Chicago Cocktail? What was Smell-O-Vision?

Welcome to Chicago!

PART I

HIDDEN LANDMARKS

A HOUSE IN FOREST PARK

The little frame cottage at 1314 South Marengo Avenue in Forest Park is tidy and nondescript, no different from others on the block and in the neighborhood. Yet there is a surprising story behind it.

William Blythe Jr. was born into a poor Texas farm family in 1918, one of nine children. As a young man, he worked as a traveling salesman for an auto parts company in Texas and nearby states. Early in 1943, he happened to bring his girlfriend into a Shreveport hospital for treatment of a minor medical problem. There he met student nurse Virginia Cassidy.

While the girlfriend was being treated, William and Virginia began talking. They hit it off. The next day, William called Virginia for a date. She accepted.

Meanwhile, World War II was raging on. Two months after meeting, William and Virginia were married. Then William went into the army.

William Blythe's civilian job got him assignment as a motor pool mechanic. He served in Egypt and Italy, earning sergeant's stripes, until the war ended in the summer of 1945. That December, he was discharged. He had been in the army thirty-two months.

Now reunited, William and Virginia decided to settle in Chicago. They arrived in the city early in 1946. While William looked for work, they lived in a single room at the Harrison Hotel, just south of the Loop.

William and Virginia Blythe's prospective Forest Park home. *Photograph by the author.*

Virginia soon discovered she was pregnant. She returned to live with her parents in her hometown of Hope, Arkansas, while William remained in Chicago, continuing his job search. In April, he was hired by a West Side auto parts company.

Housing was in short supply in 1946. New home construction had been suspended during the war, and now millions of ex–service personnel were suddenly looking for places to live. In May, William found the vacant house on Marengo Avenue in Forest Park. He bought it and called Virginia to tell her the good news.

William Blythe spent the next several days in a frenzy of activity. He cleaned the house, stocked it with furniture, arranged to have the electricity and gas turned on. Then, on the morning of May 17, he set out in his Buick to bring his wife back to their new home. Ahead of him lay 770 miles of pre-interstate America.

Late that first night, William was traveling along U.S. 60 near Sikeston, Missouri. As he rounded a curve, the right front tire of the Buick blew. The car skidded on the wet pavement, went off the road, and flipped over. With no seat belt, William was thrown out of the car.

What happened after that can only be surmised. Perhaps William landed in a roadside drainage ditch filled with rainwater. Perhaps he landed on the road after the crash, got up, and then fell into the ditch. The next morning, police came upon the scene and found William Blythe dead in the ditch. He had drowned in three feet of water.

"Veteran Killed in Crash on Way to Meet Wife" the headline read on the *Chicago Tribune*'s May 19 report of William's death. The story was told in a single paragraph, a bit of filler amid the news of a busy metropolis. An army sergeant who'd safely come through the deadliest war in history had been killed in a freak accident. It was a sad little tale.

William Blythe's body was returned to his grieving widow in Hope. After funeral services there, his remains were sent to Texas for burial in the family plot at Sherman.

Now, for the rest of the story—

Virginia Blythe decided to stay in Arkansas after her husband's death. Their son was born on August 19, 1946, and named after his late father. The house in Forest Park was sold. It is not known whether Virginia ever saw it.

In 1950, Virginia Blythe remarried. Her son later adopted his stepfather's last name. William Blythe's posthumous son eventually became the forty-second president of the United States—Bill Clinton.

The house on Marengo Avenue is a private residence. It is not known whether President Clinton ever saw it.

THE WANDERING CHURCH

Our Lady of Lourdes Parish was founded to serve English-speaking Catholics in the Ravenswood neighborhood in 1892. The initial congregation was ninety families. A frame church was quickly built on the southwest corner of Ashland and Leland Avenues.

In 1907, the Ravenswood Branch of the North Side 'L' began operation. Residential construction soon followed, and the population swelled. Though another Catholic parish was organized a mile to the west, the little wooden Our Lady of Lourdes Church was becoming overcrowded.

In 1913, the pastor concluded that a bigger church was needed. The architectural firm of Worthmann & Steinbach presented plans for a Spanish Romanesque building to be erected on the east side of Ashland and received the commission. Construction began early in 1914. By the end of 1915, the work was finished.

The new Catholic archbishop, George Mundelein, officially dedicated the new Our Lady of Lourdes Church on May 21, 1916. So far, so good. Then the growing city once again intruded.

As Chicago moved through the 1920s, more and more automobiles were clogging the streets. The city had already begun widening a few select arterials. Now the pace quickened. Among the streets to be widened was Ashland Avenue.

Ashland was a standard sixty-six feet wide. To increase its width to one hundred feet, seventeen feet would be lopped off on each side of the street. That usually meant taking some private property by eminent domain. Buildings that were already in place would have to be cut back or completely demolished.

Our Lady of Lourdes had been built to face Ashland Avenue. Truncating part of the front entrance was not possible. The only alternatives were to tear down the church or move it to another site.

Father James Scanlan had been appointed pastor in 1914. After ten years, he'd finally cleared the parish of the construction debt. Now he decided that the best solution to the current problem was to move the entire building across Ashland to the original site of the frame church, the southwest corner with Leland.

Our Lady of Lourdes Church, current location. *Photograph by the author.*

Father Scanlan announced the project in July 1928. The cost was put at $300,000—over $5 million in today's money. As the first stage of fundraising, the parish held a picnic at Kolze's Grove on Irving Park Boulevard. On September 6, work began on digging the foundation at the new site.

The task of moving the church itself began the following March. The ten-thousand-ton structure was jacked off its existing foundation and placed on steel rails that acted as rollers. Ashland Avenue was closed to traffic. Then, very slowly, fifty men, two tractors, and two teams of horses began taking the building on its four-hundred-foot journey. One member of the crew joked that the church was speeding at "one foot per minute."

The move across Ashland took five days. Once the church had crossed Ashland, it was rotated ninety degrees to face Leland. The building was also cut in half and separated. A thirty-foot-wide addition was inserted between the two sections to increase the sanctuary's capacity.

While work moving the church was in progress, Our Lady of Lourdes parishioners attended services in the parish school or at the Rainbo Gardens dining room a few blocks away. In March 1929, the relocated church was reopened. And on October 6, Archbishop Mundelein—by now Cardinal Mundelein—once again came out to dedicate Our Lady of Lourdes, this time at its latest site.

The relocation of Our Lady of Lourdes was hailed as one of the great engineering feats of the 1920s. It was considered yet another example of the "I Will" spirit that Chicago's boosters loved to celebrate. About the only discordant note was humorously struck by *Tribune* columnist Fred Pasley, who wondered if Father Scanlan would still be able to watch the baseball games in Chase Park from the church's new site.

Our Lady of Lourdes Church has now remained in place for nearly a century. However, in 2021, declining population convinced the Catholic archdiocese to consolidate the parish with St. Mary of the Lake Parish in Uptown. At this writing, the future of "the wandering church" at Ashland and Leland is uncertain.

RESTRICTIVE COVENANT

In the spring of 1937, Carl Hansberry purchased a three-flat at 6140 South Rhodes Avenue. He moved in with his family on the morning of June 15. The trouble started that evening.

Hansberry, his wife, and their children were sitting in the living room with some friends when two bricks smashed through the front window. No one was hurt. The police were called, and they posted a guard around the property.

Carl Hansberry was a Black man moving into an all-White neighborhood. In those times, in many parts of America, that was enough to provoke violence.

In 1884, the Washington Park Race Track opened on Chicago's South Side. It occupied a parcel of land just south of Washington Park, bounded by 60th Street, Cottage Grove Avenue, 63rd Street, and South Park Avenue. After the track closed in 1905, the property was subdivided and developed, becoming known as the Washington Park Subdivision. The Hansberry three-flat was located there.

African Americans were already living west of South Park Avenue in 1937. Before Carl Hansberry moved in, none were living east of that street. Two days after the attack on his home, six of Hansberry's new neighbors filed suit against him for $100,000 in the Circuit Court of Cook County. He was accused of engaging in a conspiracy to violate a restrictive covenant.

A restrictive covenant is a clause in a contract that requires one party to do—or to refrain from doing—certain things. When the previous owner had purchased the Rhodes three-flat, the contract said, "No part of said premises shall in any manner be used or occupied by a Negro or Negroes." An exception was made for "janitors, chauffeurs, or house servants." Racist restrictions like these were not uncommon at that time.

To the east of Cottage Grove Avenue, the Woodlawn and Hyde Park neighborhoods were all-White. Many people there saw the subdivision as a buffer zone to keep out Black people. The restrictive covenant used in the subdivision was the work of a group called the Woodlawn Property Owners' Association.

Hansberry was a real estate broker and political activist. He was also secretary of the Chicago branch of the National Association for the Advancement of Colored People. The NAACP was already involved in fighting restrictive covenants in other parts of the country. Hansberry decided to take his case to court.

Meanwhile, hostile mobs continued to gather outside his home. Mrs. Hansberry often spent the night patrolling the property with a loaded pistol.

The Circuit Court ruled against Hansberry, ordering his family to move. The decision was appealed to the Illinois Supreme Court. Again, the restrictive covenant was upheld. The only place left to go was the United States Supreme Court.

Carl Hansberry's
prospective home
on Rhodes Avenue.
Photograph by the author.

Anna M. Lee was one of the White signers of the restrictive covenant. Now the U.S. Supreme Court agreed to hear the case of *Hansberry v. Lee*. In a unanimous decision, the court ruled in favor of Hansberry on November 13, 1940.

The Hansberry decision is considered a civil rights landmark. However, the Supreme Court ruled only on the technical aspects of this particular restrictive covenant in this particular case. The justices refused to take up the constitutionality of such covenants. After spending a small fortune of his own money, Carl Hansberry was told that he could keep the building on Rhodes Avenue and live in it, if he still wished to do so.

In 1948, the U.S. Supreme Court decision in *Shelley v. Kraemer* finally declared restrictive covenants unconstitutional, as a violation of the Fourteenth

Amendment's equal protection provision. Carl Hansberry did not see that day. He died in 1946.

Hansberry's youngest daughter, Lorraine, later became a celebrated writer. She was seven years old when the family moved into the Rhodes Avenue three-flat. Her most famous play, *A Raisin in the Sun*, was partly based on her childhood experiences there.

The building at 6140 South Rhodes Avenue is an official City of Chicago Landmark and is privately owned. And in a satisfying bit of historical irony, the racial boundary that Carl Hansberry dared to cross—South Park Avenue—is now named Dr. Martin Luther King Jr. Drive.

THE EVITA FROM CHICAGO

Hyde Park–Kenwood is Chicago's neighborhood of presidents. Barack Obama was living there when he was elected, and Ronald Reagan lived there for a couple of years as a boy. Go a few miles south, into the South Shore neighborhood, and you'll find another presidential home, though not of a U.S. president. The president was Janet Jagan, and the country was Guyana.

She was born Janet Rosalie Rosenberg at Michael Reese Hospital in 1920 to a middle-class Jewish family. Her father, Charles, worked as a clerk and salesman in various businesses. During Janet's childhood, the family lived at 7532 South East End Avenue, and she attended the nearby Bryn Mawr Elementary School.

"My earliest memories of Janet are just being enraptured by her," Janet's cousin Suzanne Wasserman later recalled. "She was very beautiful and very athletic. She always did so many different things." Horseback riding and swimming were among her favorite activities. Janet herself remembered going to movies at the Avalon Theater and traveling downtown to the main library with her father.

The Depression of the 1930s hit the family hard. Charles Rosenberg couldn't find work, and his wife, Kate, earned a pittance doing sewing. The family eventually left Chicago and moved to Detroit

In Detroit, Janet became involved in leftist political causes at Wayne State University. When the United States entered World War II in 1941, she returned to Chicago to attend nursing school at Cook County Hospital. There she met Cheddi Jagan.

Of East Indian descent, Cheddi was a native of the South American colony then known as British Guiana. His plantation foreman father had won a chunk of money in the national lottery, enough to send Cheddi to the United States to further his education. Now Cheddi was studying dentistry at Northwestern University.

Janet and Cheddi fell in love and married in 1943. Neither set of parents was enthusiastic about the match. "Janet's father threatened to shoot me," Cheddi later wrote.

The young couple settled in Guyana. Cheddi opened a dental practice serving mostly the working class and the poor, with Janet as his nurse. They had two children. They also became active in the country's independence movement.

In 1950, the Jagans co-founded the Peoples Progressive Party (PPP). During the next fifteen years, both Jagans were elected to various political offices. Because of their leftist activism, both spent time in prison as suspected Communist subversives. At one point, the British colonial government banned them from holding the positions of president or prime minister.

After Guyana achieved full independence in 1966, both Janet and Cheddi served in Parliament. Most of the time, Cheddi was Leader of the

President Janet Rosenberg Jagan's childhood home. *Photograph by the author.*

Opposition. In 1992, the PPP won a majority of votes, and he became the country's fourth president. He died in office of a heart attack in 1997.

Nine days after Cheddi's death, Janet was sworn in as Guyana's prime minister by the new president. It was widely expected that she would run for president herself at the next election later in the year. Back in Chicago, local newspapers began running stories about the Jewish grandmother from the South Side who was likely to become Guyana's next president.

In December, Janet Jagan was elected president with 56 percent of the vote. However, the opposition People's National Congress claimed that the election had been rigged, leading to a series of protests. To calm the situation, Janet announced that she would step down after three years of her five-year term, opening the way for a new election.

Janet had said she did not want to be president but was only running for the office to continue Cheddi's legacy. In August 1999, less than two years into her term, she resigned the office due to a heart condition. Though out of office, she remained involved in politics until her death on March 28, 2009.

Suzanne Wasserman wrote and directed a documentary film on her cousin Janet's life titled *Thunder in Guyana* in 2003. The house on East End Avenue where Janet Rosenberg Jagan grew up is a private residence.

NOTRE DAME'S FIGHTING NORWEGIAN

When Knute Rockne entered the University of Notre Dame as a freshman in 1910, he was twenty-two years old and trying to find his way in life after being kicked out of high school. Notre Dame itself was an obscure little Catholic college in South Bend, Indiana. By the time he was killed in a 1931 plane crash, both Rockne and Notre Dame were celebrated throughout America.

Football had done it. As a player, Rockne had helped change the game by using the forward pass to beat a heavily favored Army team. Then, as a coach, he'd led the Fighting Irish to three national championships while compiling a 105-12-5 record, still the best in college or pro football history.

Before Rockne went off to Notre Dame and glory, he lived in Chicago. His onetime home is located at 2521 North Rockwell Street.

Knute Rockne was born in 1888 in the Norwegian municipality of Voss. His father, Lars, was a blacksmith. A few years later, Lars struck out alone for Chicago and the well-paying jobs setting up for the 1893 Columbian Exposition. Lars liked what he saw in Chicago and sent for his family.

The Rocknes settled into the brick house on Rockwell Street in 1893. The neighborhood had a significant number of Norwegians and various institutions to serve them, including a Norwegian-language newspaper. Lars got a job selling papers and keeping the printing presses in order.

Knute Rockne attended Brentano Elementary School for eight years. A bright student with a remarkable memory, he enjoyed reading and excelled in history and geography. He earned extra money washing windows and weeding gardens.

In 1901, Knute entered Northwest Division (later Tuley) High School. He began to take a greater interest in athletics. Still too small for a spot on the football team, he concentrated on track and field events his first three years.

He finally made the school football team his senior year. The sport was still in its infancy, the schedule haphazard, with games booked or canceled on short notice. Reports on Northwestern Division's 1904 season are sketchy. About the only thing that's known of Rockne's role is that he played end.

With his detour into football over, Rockne went back to his first love, track and field. His best event was the half-mile run, and he began to acquire a local reputation. The Chicago Athletic Association recruited him for its junior team.

In the spring of 1905, Rockne and some of his track teammates were working out in Humboldt Park when they were supposed to be in class. The principal spotted them and disbanded the team. The guilty parties were expelled from Northwest Division. Rockne was given the option of finishing his senior year at another high school. But his low grades made it unlikely he'd be admitted to his college of choice, the University of Chicago. So he went to work.

He spent the next year doing various odd jobs. In 1907, he took the civil service exam for the U.S. Post Office and passed. Shortly after his nineteenth birthday, Rockne went to work as a clerk at the main Chicago post office. A few months later, he was promoted to dispatcher.

However, Rockne had not completely given up on college. He wanted to be a pharmacist. Notre Dame did not have as stringent entrance requirements as other schools and didn't care that he hadn't gotten his high school diploma. So he went off to South Bend.

Rockne studied chemistry. He competed in track, and in his sophomore year, he joined the football team. Then, in May 1912, his father suddenly died. Knute was ready to quit school and return home to support the family.

Knute Rockne's Chicago home. *Photograph by the author.*

But his sisters took a long-range view and talked him out of it. The family moved off Rockwell Street into a smaller house, and Knute continued with his studies—and with football.

The City of Chicago has honored the football legend with Knute Rockne Stadium, at 1117 South Central Avenue. Though the realtor mentioned the Rockne connection when the Rockwell Street home went up for sale a while ago, there is as yet no Marker of Distinction on the property.

LOUIS AND LIL ARMSTRONG HOME

Louis Armstrong arrived at Chicago's 12th Street Station from New Orleans on an August night in 1922. Joe "King" Oliver had invited Armstrong to join his Creole Jazz Band as second cornet. Armstrong had just turned twenty-one.

Oliver was supposed to meet his protégé at the station. Unfortunately, Armstrong had missed his train, and Oliver couldn't wait around. But King had paid one of the porters to be on the lookout for a particular young man. The porter took charge of Armstrong and hustled him into a cab. Fifteen minutes later, Oliver was introducing him to the rest of the band at the Lincoln Gardens Café.

A few days later, Oliver introduced Armstrong to another member of the band, the pianist, Lil Hardin. Armstrong had earlier seen a photograph of the young lady and was impressed. When the two met, Hardin was not impressed. "Everything he had on was too small for him," she later wrote. "His atrocious tie was dangling down over his protruding stomach, and to top it off, he had a hairdo that called for bangs." This Louis Armstrong was nothing but a hick.

Then Lil heard Louis play. She saw that he had a raw, natural talent. The two of them bonded over music. Their bond soon developed into romance.

Lil began to take charge of Louis. Her first job was to change his appearance. She got him to buy new clothes, and she showed him how to wear them. She took him to a barber who gave him a better hairstyle.

She also counseled Louis in professional matters. King Oliver had been Louis's mentor in New Orleans and had brought him to Chicago. He still treated Louis like a child. Lil thought that Oliver felt threatened by his protégé's greater talent and was keeping Louis in the background.

Armstrong had married a New Orleans woman named Daisy Parker when he was eighteen. The marriage had fallen apart. He was still married to Daisy when he came to Chicago, though they had not lived together for two years. Armstrong filed for divorce in the fall of 1923. The final decree was granted two days before Christmas. Six weeks later, Louis and Lil were wed.

The new couple moved into an eleven-room graystone townhouse at 421 East 44th Street, just off fashionable Grand Boulevard. Lil's widowed mother moved in with them. Lil had scouted out the property before the wedding and made sure that the title was listed in her name. She decorated and furnished the house to suit her taste. Her new husband's main contribution was a baby grand piano.

All along, Louis's reputation as a performer had been growing and spreading. Lil knew that he would never reach his full potential playing second fiddle—er, second trumpet. She cajoled and threatened him to move on from King Oliver. Louis gave Oliver notice in June 1924. However, Lil remained with the band. "One of us has got to be working," she said.

That October, Fletcher Henderson offered Louis a spot as first trumpet in his orchestra in New York. Though the money wasn't very good, the prestige made up for it. Leaving Lil behind in Chicago, Louis went off to New York. He stayed with Henderson a little more than a year. By the end of 1925, Louis was back in Chicago. Lil had gotten him an engagement at

Louis and Lil Armstrong's home. *Photograph by the author.*

the Dreamland Café for a hefty seventy-five dollars a week. He was billed as "The World's Greatest Trumpet Player."

While his professional life was advancing, his personal life was in crisis. "With all that swell home Lil and I had, there was no happiness there," Louis later said. "We were always fussing and threatening to break up." He became involved with a young lady named Alpha Smith. Louis moved out of the house on 44th Street, though he continued to be married to Lil. When the couple finally divorced in 1938, Alpha became his third wife.

Louis Armstrong died in 1971. His longtime New York City home, in the Corona section of Queens, is now the Louis Armstrong House Museum. His Chicago home on 44th Street remains a private residence.

CHARLIE WEBER HOME

The house on the northeast corner of Addison and Wolcott is hard to miss. The buildings along this stretch of Addison are 1920s two-flats and even older frame cottages, except for this one, a postwar yellow brick bi-level home, set back behind a brick perimeter fence. This is where Charlie Weber lived—and where he died.

Charlie Weber was a politician. Born in 1894, he grew up in the North Side German neighborhood along Lincoln Avenue, where his family owned a saloon. In 1922, he was elected to the Illinois House. More importantly, in 1926 he became Forty-Fifth Ward Democratic committeeman.

Weber's duchy took in most of the city's established German area. His headquarters was a *bierstube* next to St. Alphonsus Church on Southport Avenue. During the 1930s, Weber won a seat on the Cook County Board. After a single term there, he went back to being a state rep. The years passed. By the 1950s, Weber and his buddy Paddy Bauler had become known as the last of the old-school saloonkeeper politicos. In 1955, Weber gave up his seat in Springfield and was elected Forty-Fifth Ward alderman.

Throughout Weber's career, the voters of his ward had the uncomfortable habit of casting too many Republican votes. Now that he was back in Chicago full time, the new alderman decided the best way to make his constituents happy was personal service—lots of it.

Weber had a mania for keeping the ward clean. Besides the regular city crews, he hired his own fleet of street sweepers. He also had a snowplow and a leaf-burner hauled around by a vintage Rolls-Royce. Every Christmas,

Weber threw a party for the ward's trash collectors, his "Knights of Cleanliness." Long before it was an accepted custom, he lectured dog owners about picking up their pets' excrement.

Sometimes his service was truly personal. In one incident, a housewife called the ward office to say there was a dead rat lying on the sidewalk in front of her house. A few minutes later, Alderman Weber drove up in his Cadillac, scooped the dead rodent into a gunnysack, and drove away.

Weber also cultivated future voters. He organized a group of 150 pre-teens into a club as deputy aldermen. He built and equipped seven playgrounds in the ward. And every summer there was Charlie Weber Kids Day at the Riverview amusement park. Close to 50,000 kids would be given the run of the place, while the alderman walked through the crowds passing out silver dollars.

The 1960 Kids Day was shaping up to be the greatest yet. Weber had invited Democratic vice presidential candidate Lyndon Johnson to attend as guest of honor. While waiting for Johnson's response, the alderman attended a political meeting on the evening of August 15. The meeting broke up at 11:30 p.m., and he left for home.

The next day, a friend phoned Weber and didn't receive an answer. After repeated calls, the man went to the house to investigate. He found the

Alderman Charlie Weber's house, as seen from the attached garage. *Photograph by the author.*

alderman and his wife lying dead on the floor. Carbon monoxide poisoning had caused the deaths. The Weber home had an attached garage. One of the cars had the key in the ignition and an empty gas tank. It seemed likely that Weber had forgotten to turn off the engine before going to bed. The fumes then seeped into the house through the air-conditioning ducts.

Charlie Weber's sudden death gave rise to dozens of conspiracy theories. Some observers said it had been a mob hit. Others claimed that Charlie had been blackmailing higher-level politicians. One bizarre scenario said that the Webers had been killed because the alderman had opposed John F. Kennedy's nomination for president—never mind that Weber was now working overtime for the Kennedy-Johnson ticket. The car-engine-left-running explanation was too pat, just as the lone-assassin-in-the-book-depository explanation for Kennedy's assassination would be too pat.

One urban legend is easily disposed of. The sale of Chicago homes with attached garages did not plummet after Charlie Weber's death.

The Webers had no children. Today, the house at 3601 North Wolcott Avenue is a private residence.

PART II

DRIVE-BY NEIGHBORHOODS

UPTOWN

Uptown! The name seems more generic than specific. And the district the city calls Community Area 3 did start out as a number of separate communities.

During the 1850s, two rival railroads—the Milwaukee Road and the Chicago & North Western—built parallel lines north from Chicago. Where the railroads opened stations, settlement sprang up. Buena Park was about five miles north of Madison Street. Moving farther north up the lake shore, there was a community known as Sheridan Park and, north of that, another called Edgewater. All three of these settlements were annexed by Chicago in 1889.

In 1909, the first North Side 'L' line pushed through the area to a terminal at Wilson Avenue. Rapid growth followed. The three distinct communities lost their separate identities and blended together. By the 1920s, the whole area was referred to as Uptown.

Why "Uptown"? If you think about it, that was pretty savvy marketing. The name tried to put the community on the same level as Downtown, aka the Loop. The main local business street also adopted a more cosmopolitan identity—Evanston Avenue became Broadway. In New York, Midtown was outpacing the city's older business areas. The same thing could happen in Chicago. Uptown boosters predicted that one day, the Broadway Limited would locate its Chicago terminal at Wilson Avenue.

It seemed possible in the 1920s. Department stores, banks, hotels, and every manner of business were moving in. You could find or do almost anything in Uptown. Even Al Capone was investing in local real estate.

People from all over Chicago came to Uptown for entertainment. The action centered on the Broadway-Lawrence intersection. The major movie palaces included the Riviera and the four-thousand-seat Uptown, the city's largest. For dancing, there was the Aragon Ballroom. The Green Mill was the place to go for hot jazz, and over on Clark Street, the Rainbo Gardens complex offered assorted cabaret shows.

After a busy Saturday night, there were churches available. All Saints Episcopal and Our Lady of the Lake Catholic were architectural treasures. The biggest congregation gathered at the People's Church, where celebrated Unitarian pastor Preston Bradley held forth. Summer Sundays might also include a visit to Lake Michigan for fishing off the Horseshoe, or swimming at Montrose Beach, or golf at the nearby Waveland Golf Course, the "poor man's Pebble Beach."

And when you died, you could still find what you needed in Uptown. Graceland Cemetery, the city's most fashionable burying ground, was located in the community.

The Crash of '29 and the Depression hit Uptown hard. Businesses died and money left. Large apartments were carved into rooming houses. Poorer

Uptown—still waiting for the Broadway Limited at Uptown Station. *Photograph by the author.*

people moved in. The newcomers included African Americans, Native Americans, and Appalachian Whites.

By 1970, portions of Wilson Avenue had become a skid row. The crime rate soared, and 'L' commuters were warned not to change trains at area stations. Uptown's reputation was getting so bad that residents north of Foster Avenue petitioned city officials to secede. The request was granted, and today, that neighborhood is designated a separate community area, #77—Edgewater.

Still, some sections of Uptown remained intact. These were mostly on the outer edges, near the Chicago & North Western tracks or along Marine Drive. Two blocks of Hutchinson Street were designated an architectural landmark district. The construction of Truman College off Wilson Avenue helped stabilize the central area.

In the 1980s, things seemed to be turning around. To the south, Wrigleyville and Boys' Town were attracting young urban professionals. Gentrification seemed certain to spread into Uptown. And that became the new hot-button political issue.

Various groups organized protests against the creeping change. They claimed that "urban renewal" simply meant "poor removal." In 1987, local activist Helen Shiller was elected to the city council from the Forty-Sixth Ward. More recently the speed of gentrification has slowed, and community leaders seek to balance the needs of the different constituencies.

The 2020 census reported that Uptown had a total population of 57,182. It remains one of the city's most diverse areas. A little more than half of those counted are identified as White non-Hispanics. African Americans make up about 18 percent of the total population, with Hispanics at 15 percent and Asians at 10 percent.

SOUTH CHICAGO

North Chicago is in Lake County. West Chicago is in Du Page County. East Chicago is in Indiana. But where is South Chicago?

South Chicago is part of the City of Chicago, about ten miles southeast of the Loop. Officially designated as Community Area 46, it's roughly triangular in shape, bounded by 79th Street, South Chicago Avenue, and Lake Michigan.

If Jefferson Davis had been listened to, this location might have become downtown Chicago. In 1833, as a young army officer, Davis surveyed the various rivers that could be linked to the planned Illinois and Michigan Canal. He said that the Calumet River was the best choice. Speculators began buying up land in the area. Then the politicians picked the Chicago River as the link to the canal. The Calumet River boom went bust. For the next few decades, growth here was slow. A few scattered settlements developed. The biggest of them was Ainsworth. By 1867, when the Village of Hyde Park annexed the area, the name "South Chicago" was coming into common use.

Enter James Bowen, often called the Father of South Chicago. In 1869, Bowen organized a company to develop the Calumet River and its harbor. The company also began buying land, subdividing it, and laying out streets.

Did Bowen know something? The very next year, Congress made a major appropriation to deepen the Calumet River.

A handful of industries had been located in South Chicago. As the harbor was improved, more industry came. And with lumberyards and iron forges and grain elevators going up, railroads started laying track to serve them. And with railroads coming in, even more industry was attracted to the area, and—well, you can see where this is going.

The one industry that made South Chicago was steel. The big daddy of the steel plants was South Works, opened on the lakefront near 91st Street in 1881. By 1901, the facility stretched all the way north to 79th Street. That was the year it became part of the new U.S. Steel Corporation.

South Chicago was annexed by Chicago in 1889. The community then had about twenty-four thousand people, and more were on the way. Many of these settlers were Poles and other Eastern Europeans.

Housing was built quickly and cheaply. The blocks near South Works were divided into "shoestring lots" (140 feet long but only 25 feet wide) and crammed with frame cottages and two-flats. The result was the worst living conditions in Chicago. The steel mill that provided jobs also fouled the air and deafened the ears. The land itself was low and swampy. One writer described the area as having "pools of water, ditches clogged with soot, garbage, and industrial debris, [as well as] decomposed animals."

When sewers were finally built in these areas, the simplest method was to lay the sewers along the ground and then pave over them. This raised the level of some streets fourteen feet or more—and the first floor of many houses now became the basement. You can still see evidence of these "sunken homes" along Houston Avenue and other streets.

South Chicago, with sunken homes along Houston Avenue. *Photograph by the author.*

The northern sections of South Chicago remained vacant until the 1920s, when brick bungalows began going up. Population growth continued, peaking at fifty-six thousand in 1930. Now the residents included many Mexicans, with a sprinkling of African Americans. The blocks around 92nd and Commercial became a major commercial district; locals referred to it as "Downtown."

South Chicago was made by steel. At one time, about 70 percent of the adult men were employed in the steel industry, at South Works or other plants in nearby communities. The Chicago-Gary corridor was the steel-producing center of the world.

The American steel industry declined after World War II. The reasons why this happened have been debated at length. South Chicago suffered through the decline. The final blow came in 1992, when South Works closed for good.

Today, the community is trying to rebound. The 2020 census counted about twenty-seven thousand residents. The population is about 75 percent African American, the rest mostly Hispanic. Ambitious plans are going forward to develop the vacant South Works land. And once again, this site may be the key to the future of South Chicago.

HUMBOLDT PARK

Humboldt Park is a large 207-acre park on the West Side. Humboldt Park is also Chicago Community Area 23 on the West Side.

Humboldt Park (the park) is not located in Humboldt Park.

The official community boundaries were drawn up by University of Chicago scholars in the 1920s. They decided that the park was part of the West Town neighborhood. Why they did this is too complicated to explain here. To keep things from getting confusing, I'm going to refer to the community area as HP.

In 1869, Chicago annexed much of the current West Side. Work also began that year on building the three great West Side parks. HP, the area west of Humboldt Park, was mostly prairie. The few settlers were connected to the city by Whiskey Point Road (now called Grand Avenue—why did they ever change that name?).

The Great Fire of 1871 caused Chicago to adopt new building laws. HP was part of the city but outside the fire code limits. Low-cost frame houses could still be built there. Several developers moved in. Most of the new residents were blue-collar. Many were employed at the Chicago & North Western Railway's 40th Avenue Shops or in factories along the Belt Line Railroad to the west. Germans and Scandinavians were most numerous.

More people moved in when streetcar lines arrived in the 1890s. Block after block of cottages were built. They followed a few simple designs and looked very similar. More often than you'd think possible, residents would get confused and try to enter the wrong house.

North Avenue, which had both a streetcar and an 'L' line, became the main shopping street. The area around North and Crawford (Pulaski) had several banks, theaters, and restaurants. Two-flats and apartment buildings lined the surrounding side streets.

HP's population reached eighty thousand in 1930. The Germans and Scandinavians had now been joined by Poles, Italians, and Russian Jews. One observer noted that these diverse groups all got along well with one another—unlike their compatriots in Europe, who would soon be fighting World War II.

Well into the 1950s, HP looked much the same. The number of residents leveled off at about seventy-five thousand. People had jobs, and the stores did good business. Yet times were changing, as seen by the fate of the local 'L' line.

The Humboldt Park 'L' was a branch of the Logan Square main line. It ran over the alley north of North Avenue as far west as Lawndale Avenue.

Humboldt Park, the unofficial boundary marker on Humboldt Boulevard. *Photograph by the author.*

There were plans to extend the line farther west, as traffic dictated. But instead, the number of riders started dropping. In 1952, the CTA shut down the line.

The most traumatic local event of the 1950s was the fire at Our Lady of the Angels School in 1958. The blaze killed ninety-two children and three nuns and tore the heart out of the area around Chicago and Hamlin.

During the 1960s, the ethnic makeup of HP began changing. Hispanics moved into the eastern section. The earliest settlers were Puerto Rican, with sizeable numbers of Mexicans coming later. In the blocks south of Chicago Avenue, African Americans became a majority.

At the same time, Chicago's economy was evolving. Thousands of manufacturing jobs left the city. In HP, many small factories closed. So did big plants like Helene Curtis Cosmetics and Schwinn Bicycles. The city created an industrial park on abandoned railroad land near Chicago and Pulaski. A new municipal incinerator was built on the site, along with warehouses, factories, a CTA garage, and Orr High School. However, many parcels within the property still remained vacant.

Economic uncertainty brought tough times to HP. During the late 1970s, an arson epidemic devastated the community. As vandalism and violent crime rose, more businesses left. Courtesy Motors, at one time the city's leading auto dealer, shut its doors for good.

HP has spent the last three decades hanging on. New construction has taken place in fits and starts. The 2020 census reported a population of about fifty-four thousand. Most of that number was identified as either Hispanic or African American.

BRIGHTON PARK

Brighton Park is a Southwest Side neighborhood located about seven miles from the Loop along Archer Avenue. It is officially designated as Chicago Community Area 58.

There are at least three different stories on how Brighton Park got its name. Some sources say that Brighton Park was named for the city of Brighton in England. Others say it was named after the Brighton Livestock Market in Boston. A few historians insist that the area's name derives from the Brighton Park Race Track, owned by Chicago politician Long John Wentworth.

What's agreed on is that settlement began in the 1830s, during construction of the Illinois and Michigan Canal. The land itself wasn't very inviting. Much of the area was low-lying and marshy, with the occasional clay hole. Flooding was frequent. Still, a few truck farmers stuck it out.

Local businessman John McCaffery is called the Father of Brighton Park. Seeing possibilities where others saw swamp, he built a plank road along what is now Western Avenue and began subdividing the land to the west. In 1851, the Village of Brighton Park was incorporated.

Railroads entered soon afterward. Various industries were established. Brighton Park had a nail factory, a brickyard, a cotton mill, and even a stockyard. One of the biggest plants made blasting powder—until a lightning strike blew up the place.

Brighton Park became part of Chicago in the great annexation of 1889. Yet as it developed, the community was cut off from the rest of the city on three sides. On the north was the Sanitary and Ship Canal, successor to the Illinois and Michigan. On the west were the massive yards of the Santa Fe Railroad. On the south was an industrial park.

That isolation didn't halt the wave of settlement. The meatpackers were always hiring at the Union Stock Yards, only a short streetcar ride away. There were also plenty of jobs around locally, particularly after the Crane Plumbing Company opened its new plant in 1915. Cottages and two-flats began going up along the side streets. Archer Avenue became a thriving commercial strip.

The new people were mainly Poles, with a sprinkling of Lithuanians. The population of Brighton Park reached forty-six thousand in 1930. At that time, 37 percent of the residents identified themselves as Polish, the largest concentration of that group in the city.

For much of the twentieth century, the community was solid and stable. True, the population was dropping every decade and was recorded as thirty thousand in 1980—a decline of one-third over the course of fifty years. That was explained as due to normal aging and the vogue for smaller families. Brighton Park looked the same as always.

In 1979, a reigning pope came to Chicago for the first time. John Paul II was Polish, and he made it a point to visit his fellow countrymen at Five Holy Martyrs Parish in Brighton Park. After he left, a portion of 43rd Street was renamed Pope John Paul II Drive.

Brighton Park began changing during the 1980s. The Crane plant had closed in 1977, and now other factories started shutting down. The railroads scaled back as trucking cut into their freight business. With the decline of heavy industry, most of the residents worked in clerical or service jobs.

There were other demographic changes. In 1980, about 15 percent of Brighton Park residents identified as Hispanic. By 2020, that figure had

Brighton Park, as mentioned in this newspaper ad after annexation by Chicago. *From Chicago Tribune, March 23, 1890.*

risen to over 80 percent. The population count had rebounded to forty-five thousand, near the historic high.

Today, the Orange Line 'L' cuts through the edge of Brighton Park, giving the community easier access to the rest of the city. Some factories remain, while others have been replaced with new housing and new strip malls. There are fewer Polish restaurants and many more serving Mexican food.

The neighborhood also faces the usual urban challenges. Crime and unemployment are too high. The housing stock is growing older. There aren't enough recreational facilities, and the schools could be better.

Would John McCaffery recognize Brighton Park? Probably not. But he'd be proud of the place, just the same.

SOUTH LAWNDALE, AKA LITTLE VILLAGE

Our subject is Community Area 30, the area of the West Side generally centered on 26th Street and Central Park Avenue. Historically, the neighborhood has been known as South Lawndale. That's still the official name. But around 1964, community leaders here began referring to their turf as Little Village. North Lawndale was going through some bad times, and the people south of the Burlington Railroad wanted to emphasize their separate status. To keep the narration simple, I'm calling this area SLLV.

In 1869, the City of Chicago annexed most of the land that would become SLLV. The only hints of civilization then were a few farms and a little settlement near the Burlington tracks. That would soon change.

The Great Fire of 1871 wiped out downtown Chicago. The McCormick Reaper Works on the lakefront was among the properties destroyed. The company rebuilt on the outskirts of the city, at Western and Blue Island Avenues. When employees at the new plant began settling nearby, developers began subdividing in SLLV.

Over the next thirty years, the community grew slowly and steadily. Many of the residents were Czechs moving west from Pilsen. There were also some Germans and Poles. In 1889, the city annexed the area west of Crawford Avenue (Pulaski Road), giving SLLV its current boundaries.

The real building boom came with the new century. In 1903, the massive Hawthorne Works, builder of telephone equipment, opened just to the west in Cicero. To the north, the Douglas Park 'L' line was being extended. Cottages, two-flats, and distinctive three-decker flats began filling up the

South Lawndale/Little Village—gateway on 26th Street. *Photograph by the author.*

twenty-five-foot lots of SLLV. A ribbon commercial strip took hold along the 26th Street streetcar line.

Meanwhile, other factories and rail yards were being constructed along the community's eastern and western borders. The Sanitary and Ship Canal was built along the southern periphery and attracted similar development. SLLV became an island surrounded by a sea of industry.

The population reached eighty-four thousand in 1920, making SLLV one of the most densely packed communities in Chicago. The residents were mainly blue collar and Czech.

The most prominent resident was Anton Cermak, businessman and political boss. As president of the Cook County Board, Cermak's clout was responsible for getting the county courthouse and jail complex moved from the Near North Side to SLLV. In 1931, he was elected mayor of Chicago but was killed two years later by a shooter aiming at President-elect Franklin D. Roosevelt. Cermak's former home still stands at 2348 South Millard Avenue, a private residence.

From Cermak's time into the 1960s, SLLV didn't change much. The population steadily declined to about sixty thousand, which was a blessing. Poles replaced Czechs as the dominant nationality. A few African Americans lived in the northeast section. There were also a small number of Hispanics.

The last-named group proved to be the future of SLLV. In 1970, about a third of the population was Hispanic, and by 1980, that proportion had become 74 percent. At the same time, the total number of residents began rising again. The 1980 census counted seventy-five thousand people living in Community Area 30. Twenty years later, the population reached a historic high of ninety-one thousand.

Today, SLLV is home to about seventy-two thousand people. The 2020 census identified the population as 88 percent Hispanic, with 9 percent African American and 3 percent White. The Mexican community is the largest in the Midwest. A high point on the calendar is the 26th Street Mexican Independence Day Parade in September.

Hawthorne Works and most of the other factories are gone, and many SLLV residents now are employed in clerical and service jobs. The 26th Street strip continues to be one of the city's busiest outlying shopping districts. Several public schools have been built or expanded to serve the area.

SLLV has always suffered from a lack of parks. Though Douglass Park is just to the north, the only facility in the community itself is Piotrowski Park on 31st Street. Perhaps some of the vacated industrial land can be devoted to recreational facilities.

NORWOOD PARK

Norwood Park, Community Area 10, is one of Chicago's railroad communities. The original settlement was planned around the Chicago and North Western commuter line. But that's not the beginning of our story.

In 1833, Mark Noble filed claim to 150 acres of land in the area. He built a frame house on a glacial ridge and lived the life of a gentleman farmer. Today, his home, at 5634 North Newark Avenue, is the oldest building in Chicago.

Other farmers followed Noble. Then, in 1868, a group of Chicago investors purchased 860 acres near the railroad for real estate development. Taking their name from a popular novel, they called their community Norwood Park. A town hall and shops were built across from the C&NW station.

The new town featured wide lots with expansive front lawns. Instead of following the rigid Chicago grid, the streets were pleasantly curved; one of them even formed a circle. Three small parks were laid out and hundreds of shade trees planted.

To promote development, frequent ads were run in the Chicago newspapers. It's worth quoting one of them: "Only eleven miles from the Court House on the Chicago & North Western, thirty minutes ride. Eighty feet above the lake on beautiful, rolling ground, perfect drainage. No malaria, no saloons, no nuisances of any kind. Good society, churches, graded schools, stores."

New settlers arrived. They built large Victorian homes on the high ground near the ridge. But as Norwood Park grew, the residents saw the need for city services. In 1893, they voted to become part of Chicago. Today, the historic heart of the original town is called Old Norwood.

The eastern part of the community was not developed until after annexation. Though closer to the city, the land here was marsh. New sewers solved that problem, and bungalows began going up.

By 1930, Norwood Park was home to fourteen thousand people. A shopping district had developed near Northwest Highway and Raven Street, and a string of small factories popped up along the railroad. Then came the Depression and World War II. Building stopped, with large areas to the south and west still prairie.

The war ended in 1945, and development resumed. Now the families of the baby boom were buying cars and looking for ranch homes. The outer portions of Norwood Park—Big Oaks, Union Ridge, Oriole Park—were filling up. The population reached twenty-seven thousand in 1950 and forty-one thousand ten years later.

Still, it took a while to tie Norwood Park to the city. The railroad was fast but expensive. Most residents who wanted to get downtown faced a long, slow journey, driving on surface streets or riding the Milwaukee Avenue streetcar.

The Northwest (Kennedy) Expressway was completed in 1960. The community now had convenient auto access to other areas, though traffic grows heavier each year. The O'Hare branch of the CTA Blue Line has been an alternative since 1983.

Drawing a map of Community Area 10 should not be attempted by amateurs. That's because the boundaries are so complicated. Politics is the reason, of course.

During the 1950s, Chicago wanted to establish a land connection to the new O'Hare Airport and began claiming large swaths of territory. The boundaries of Community Area 10 were stretched west to Cumberland Avenue. But in the middle of all this Chicago land, there are several blocks that refused to join the city and remain unincorporated. They are known as Norwood Park Township.

Norwood Park's onetime Village Hall. *Photograph by the author.*

Today, Norwood Park is a stable, middle-class community. Like other neighborhoods on the edge of the city, many of the residents are teachers, police officers, firefighters, and others who are required to live within Chicago. The 2020 census recorded a Norwood Park population of just over thirty-eight thousand people. More than three-quarters of the residents are identified as White, with Hispanics the next-largest group at 15 percent.

Norwood Park has some noteworthy landmarks that should be mentioned. Taft High School was the inspiration for Rydell High in the musical *Grease*. Superdawg Drive-in is featured in the book *1,000 Places to See Before You Die*. But the number-one landmark remains Mark Noble's farmhouse, now headquarters of the Norwood Park Historical Society.

PART III

SPORTS AND SPORTS PEOPLE

A DIFFERENT LEAGUE OF THEIR OWN

The 1992 film *A League of Their Own* tells the story of the All-American Girls Professional Baseball League (AAGPBL). The league was founded by Chicago Cubs owner (and chewing gum magnate) Phil Wrigley in 1943. World War II was on, many male professional ballplayers were in the service, and Major League Baseball faced an uncertain future. Geena Davis, Madonna, and Rosie O'Donnell portray composite characters based on AAGPBL players. Tom Hanks is their manager, a role based on baseball great Jimmie Foxx.

A League of Their Own was a box-office success and reawakened interest in the AAGPBL. Our story is about a lesser-known Chicago-based wartime women's baseball league—the National Girls' Baseball League (NGBL).

Forest Park roofing contractor Emery Parichy began sponsoring a women's twelve-inch softball team called the Bloomer Girls in 1937. He later helped organize similar local teams into the Metropolitan League. Then the AAGPBL began signing the Metropolitan League's best talent. In 1944, Parichy joined with Chicago Cardinals owner Charles Bidwill and politician Edwin Kolski to form the NGBL.

The AAGPBL was a hard-ball league, like men's professional baseball, and followed standard baseball rules. The teams played in various midwestern cities, stretching from Minneapolis to Fort Wayne. The NGBL continued to play softball and remained a Chicago-area league. Though a few players bounced back and forth between the two leagues, the NGBL became the home for those who preferred to keep playing softball or didn't like overnight travel.

The NGBL opened the 1944 season with five teams: Bloomer Girls, Bluebirds, Chicks, Kandy Kids, and Sparks. The next year, the Music Maids joined as the sixth team. As the league became established, its teams attracted a variety of sponsors. The Rock-Ola Manufacturing Corporation, maker of jukeboxes, backed a team. So did the Brach Candy Company. So did the Thillens Check Cashing Service. So did auto dealer (and onetime White Sox infielder) Tony Piet. And of course, so did Parichy with his Bloomer Girls.

The teams played in a number of small neighborhood stadiums. The Bloomer Girls were based at Parichy Memorial Stadium, at Harlem and Harrison in Forest Park. Among the venues in Chicago itself were Thillens Stadium (3200 West Devon Avenue), Rock-Ola Stadium (4200 North Central Avenue), Shewbridge Field (1035 West 74th Street), Bidwill Stadium (1975 East 75th Street), and Lane Stadium (2600 West Addison Street). A few games were played at Wrigley Field and Soldier Field.

Emery Parichy was NGBL treasurer, with co-founder Edwin Kolski serving as secretary. To give the league added publicity, football great Red Grange was hired as commissioner. Among the team managers were former Major League stars Woody English and Buck Weaver. Weaver had been banned from organized baseball for his "guilty knowledge" of the 1919 World Series fix. Many baseball fans considered his particular punishment unjust and welcomed his participation in the new league.

Just as the league's 1945 season drew to a close, World War II ended. Though the male major leagues would now be returning to full strength, the NGBL kept going. There was enough room for everybody. During those first postwar years, the league reported annual attendance of about 500,000 people—better than the White Sox were drawing then.

Still, there was always the need to promote. The NGBL began to feature extra added attractions at their games. One of the most popular was The King and His Court. This was a barnstorming male softball team, whose pitcher was so dominant they could play with only four men on the field.

Then there was Donkey Baseball. The game was played with all the players except the pitcher, catcher, and batter on donkeys. But after hitting the ball, the batter had to jump on a donkey to move around the bases. Needless to say, the action here was not exactly fast-paced.

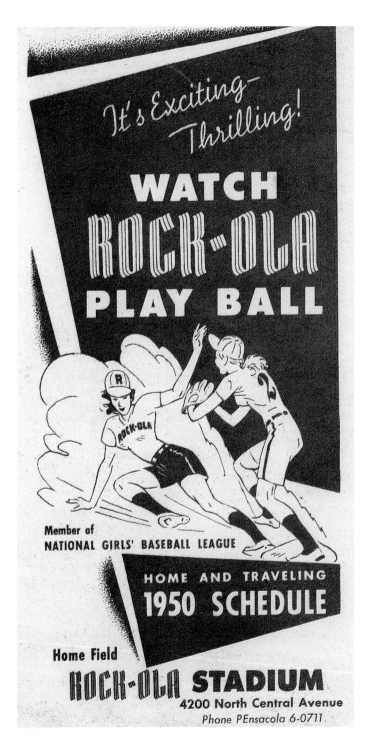

Rock-Ola's 1950 schedule folder. *Author's collection.*

Television killed women's professional baseball. By 1954, Major League Baseball broadcasts were spreading out over the country. Both the NGBL and the AAGPBL folded at the end of the season. More recently, independent filmmaker Adam Chu put together a documentary titled *Their Turn at Bat: The Story of the National Girls' Baseball League*.

LOYOLA RAMBLERS RULE!

For George Ireland, the 1962–63 basketball season did not start well. On September 7, Loyola University's longtime coach was admitted to Roosevelt Hospital with a kidney disorder. The problem turned out to be minor. He was soon released and returned to his preparations for the new season.

Ireland was optimistic. His 1961–62 Ramblers had posted a 23-4 record, with a third-place finish in the National Invitational Tournament and a #13 ranking nationally. This year's team looked even more promising.

Forward Jerry Harkness was the team's captain and leading scorer and was being talked of as a possible All-American. He was a senior. The rest of the team's starting lineup were juniors—center Les Hunter, forward Vic Rouse, and guards Ron Miller and Jack Eagan. The team played an exciting, high-scoring game.

But there was something else that made the Ramblers noteworthy. Until then, college basketball had operated under an informal rule that a team would put no more than two Black players on the court. Some schools would refuse to play against a team that had even a single Black player.

Ireland wanted to put together the strongest possible team. He actively recruited African Americans. As the new season got underway, Loyola was the only major college team to have four African American starters— Harkness, Hunter, Rouse, and Miller. And when Eagan was occasionally pulled out of the game for a breather, the team on the court might become all Black.

Loyola opened the season on December 1 with an easy victory over Christian Brothers College at Alumni Gym on campus. From there they built a 21-game winning streak until Bowling Green State stopped them in February. The Ramblers rebounded with 3 more wins, then closed the regular season with a 1-point loss to Wichita State. Their 24-2 record earned them a #5 ranking in the polls.

Then came the NCAA Tournament. In the opening round, Loyola beat Tennessee Tech 111–42—a 69-point blowout that is still the biggest victory margin in the tournament's history. Their second game would be against Mississippi State. That was causing some controversy.

For the past five years, the Mississippi State Bulldogs had declined invitations to the NCAA Tournament. The "unwritten law" of Mississippi was that White players did not compete in sporting events against Black players. Before this year's tournament began, Governor Ross Barnett issued a statement against this particular kind of integration. "It is not in the best interests of Mississippi State University, the State of Mississippi, or either of the races," he said.

Mississippi State's president ignored the governor and sent the Bulldogs to the tournament. When the Mississippi State captain shook hands with Harkness at the opening ceremony, it was obvious that times were changing— in fact, the Ramblers-Bulldogs matchup has become known in basketball lore as "The Game of Change." Loyola won, 61–51.

From there, Loyola went on to defeat Illinois and Duke in order. That put them into the title game against the University of Cincinnati Bearcats. Cincinnati had won the tournament the previous two years. They also were ranked #1 that year.

Loyola University's 1963 national basketball champs. *Courtesy of Loyola University Chicago Archives & Special Collections.*

On March 23, 1963, Loyola took to the court against Cincinnati a 25-to-1 underdog. The Bulldogs held Harkness scoreless in the first half, building up a 45–30 lead at the break. Then the Ramblers fought back. With four seconds left, Harkness sank a twelve-foot jump shot to tie the score at 54–54 and send the game into overtime.

Loyola came out fast in the five-minute overtime, grabbing a 2-point lead. Cincinnati evened the score, again Loyola grabbed the lead, and again Cincinnati caught them. But when Rouse tipped in Hunter's shot at the buzzer, the Ramblers had won an improbable 60–58 victory. Loyola became the first Illinois school to win an NCAA Division I basketball championship. Sixty years later, it is still the only one.

The 1962–63 Loyola Ramblers were inducted into the National Collegiate Basketball Hall of Fame in 2013, the first team to have that distinction. That same year, President Barack Obama honored the surviving members of the team at the White House. A documentary film on the team titled *The Loyola Project* was released in 2022.

THE FAIRWAY FLAPPER

On August 25, 1924, a golfer was featured on the cover of *Time* magazine for the first time. This particular golfer was also the first female athlete to make the cover. She was Chicago's own Edith Cummings.

Born in 1899, Cummings grew up among the city's social elite, the daughter of a banker. The family split its time between a Gold Coast townhouse and a suburban retreat in Lake Forest. At fifteen, Cummings and three other debutante friends began referring to themselves as the Big Four. The doings of the four wealthy, attractive young ladies soon became regular features on the society pages.

Both Edith's parents were accomplished golfers at the Onwentsia Club, and it was only natural that she'd take up the game. In 1918, still in her teens, she won the women's club championship. The following year, she qualified for the U.S. Women's Amateur Tournament.

There were no female golf pros yet. The Amateur was the most prestigious tournament a woman could aim to win. In 1920, Cummings again qualified at the Amateur and this time made it to the quarterfinals before losing in match play to eventual champ Alexa Stirling. At the 1922 Amateur, Cummings advanced to the semifinals. There she lost to Glenna Collett, who went on to win the title.

Cummings did win three other tournaments in 1922. Meanwhile, she was becoming a favorite with the galleries. She played aggressively and took chances. Watching Cummings in a close match, one reporter wrote that she "swaggered along like a bull-fighter, ready to pounce on any mistakes her opponent made." The male writers of the day nearly always found time to comment on her good looks.

Her personality shone through. Other star golfers—both female and male—were deadly serious. Cummings seemed to be having fun on the course. She became known as the Fairway Flapper.

Cummings summed up her attitude toward competitive golf in a December 1922 interview. "To win a national title you must make golf the be-all and end-all of your existence—you must eat, sleep, and think golf," she said. She had other interests and wanted to live a well-rounded life. "To me the game, fond as I am of it, simply isn't worth the sacrifice."

The next October, Cummings was back at the Amateur. This time, she made her way to the final match against her nemesis, three-time champion Alexa Stirling. At the halfway break of the thirty-six-hole match, Cummings was 2 down. But she fought back, closing out Stirling on the thirty-fourth green.

Cummings became a national celebrity. Her story was featured in newspapers and all the "ladies' magazines." She added to her résumé by winning the Women's Western Amateur. The *Time* cover story in August 1924 was the climax of a whirlwind year. By then, it was time for Cummings to defend her Amateur title.

But the magic was gone. Cummings was eliminated in an early round of match play. As the years passed, she played less and less competitive golf. She never won another tournament.

Cummings married businessman Curtis Munson in 1934. The couple settled in Washington, D.C. Edith continued to play recreational golf, while expanding her interests to include fishing, big-game hunting, and philanthropy. Edith Cummings Munson died in 1984.

In 1998, the Curtis and Edith Munson Foundation established the Edith Cummings Munson Award in her honor. A monetary grant is given to a female college student who combines golf skills and academic achievement. It's a fitting memorial to the award's namesake.

Besides the award, Edith has also attained a bit of indirect immortality. While she was in high school, her Big Four mate Ginevra King introduced Edith to a young Princeton student named Frank Fitzgerald. Years later, in *The Great Gatsby*, that same F. Scott Fitzgerald based the character "Daisy

Buchanan" on King and a champion golfer named "Jordan Baker" on Cummings. Trouble was, in *Gatsby*, the lady golfer is a cheater.

Nobody ever accused Edith Cummings of any rules-bending or underhanded play. Win or lose, the Fairway Flapper from Chicago was always a credit to the game.

THE BIG THREE BOWLERS TOUR

At the turn of the twentieth century, the Chicago-based Brunswick-Balke-Collender Company was the leading manufacturer of billiards equipment. Now the company was moving into an up-and-coming sport: bowling. In 1902, Brunswick executive W.V. Thompson convinced his bosses to bankroll an exhibition trip of top-flight bowlers—the Big Three Bowlers Tour.

Thompson himself was one of the country's best bowlers. Joining him as headliners were veteran kegler Fred Worden and reigning national singles champ Fred Strong. As a sub, the Big Three brought along a twenty-one-year-old farm boy who was just starting to make a name for himself, Harry Steers.

They left Chicago by train on September 28. The first stop was a three-day engagement in St. Louis. The tour's format called for the traveling trio to roll a three-game match against whatever local talent the home houses could round up. As expected, the Big Three swept the competition. Knowledgeable fans were impressed by the 1832 series the Chicagoans rolled against the Martin Kern Missouri Big Three.

From St. Louis, the tour moved west through Texas, with performances at San Antonio and El Paso. Then it was across the high plains and desert to California. Outlaw bands still roamed the wild country—New Mexico and Arizona were not yet states—and the travelers were relieved to reach Los Angeles without incident. There they rolled three matches at three different venues in a single day.

At Santa Monica, the audience was two-thirds female. Perhaps it was because the baby-faced youngster Steers was scheduled to bowl that day. In any case, the Chicagoans put on a good show. In the seventh frame of the final game, when Steers rolled a strike, Strong tossed him a silver dollar in tribute. Steers struck again in the eighth, and Worden gave him his watch. Another strike in the ninth, and Strong threw in his coat. The kid then proceeded to close with three more strikes, and his colleagues tossed him a "gift" after each ball, with Thompson capping off the fun with a fifty-dollar bill.

Santa Monica was followed by Santa Barbara before the tour moved up the coast to San Francisco. The highlight of the three days in the Bay Area was the grand opening of the new Central Alleys, where the Big Three was the featured attraction. The final California exhibition was at Stockton. Then the boys began heading home.

Once more, they went into the wilderness, this time through mountains. The one-thousand-mile journey took nearly forty hours, and the train was late getting into Denver. The Big Three barely had time to get to their engagement at the Overland Alleys. Stiff and out of practice, they lost badly to the local team. The next day, after getting acclimated, they returned to form and had no further trouble in Denver.

Lincoln, Nebraska, came next, and the Big Three posted their highest single game of the tour, 674. In Iowa, they gave performances at Carroll and Boone before arriving at Marshalltown, the boyhood home of baseball star Cap Anson. The old first baseman was now a Chicago proprietor, and Fred Worden was one of his bowling teammates. After the Big Three rolled

The Park Alley on Which the Games are Played.

One of the stops on the Big Three Bowlers Tour. *From* El Paso Herald, *October 3, 1902.*

their match, they were fêted in a special banquet, complete with welcoming speeches from Marshalltown politicians.

The last stop was Dubuque. Here the hometown team swept the match with a 1,756 series. That was the best score rolled against the Chicagoans on the tour, so Brunswick awarded each of the victors a new bowling ball and leather bag.

The Big Three Bowlers Tour lasted five weeks. During those thirty-five days, they traveled over five thousand miles and rolled forty-four separate matches. They lost only four. Thompson was the leading scorer among the regulars, averaging a shade under 188 for the trip. His 258 was also the highest single game.

After the tour, each of the Big Three continued to make news. Fred Strong won the 1903 national All Events championship. Fred Worden moved to St. Louis and managed the city's largest bowling resort. W.V. Thompson continued his distinguished career as a bowler, writer, and promoter. And little Harry Steers, the sub who'd wowed the ladies of Santa Monica, went on to become a charter member of the Bowling Hall of Fame.

THE MAN WHO MADE PRO FOOTBALL

In the fall of 1925, twenty-two-year-old Harold Grange of Wheaton was one of the most famous people in America. The public knew him as the Galloping Ghost, the Wheaton Iceman, Old Number 77, or simply Red Grange. He was a football player at the University of Illinois.

He had begun making headlines three seasons earlier. In 1923, Grange was named to Walter Camp's All-American team as a halfback, a rare honor for a sophomore. In 1924, among other accomplishments, he scored four touchdowns in the first twelve minutes against a tough Michigan team. Again he was named an All-American.

Now it was 1925. Grange was on his way to a third straight All-American season. *Time* magazine featured him on its cover. Columnist Damon Runyon wrote that Grange was "three or four men and a horse rolled into one for football purposes—Jack Dempsey, Babe Ruth, Al Jolson, Paavo Nurmi, and Man o' War." But it was all coming to an end. Grange's last football game would be on November 21, against Ohio State in Columbus.

After the Ohio State game, Grange would return to campus, go back to class, and finish his studies. Once he graduated, he might use his fame to get started in business. Or if he wanted to stay in touch with football, he could look for a coaching job. His playing days seemed to be over.

College football was the only football that mattered in 1925. The National Football League, the six-year-old professional circuit, was struggling. Though a big college game could attract seventy thousand spectators, the pros usually played before a few hundred. Most NFL players earned less than $100 a game.

During his years at the university, Grange had become acquainted with Champaign theater owner Charles C. Pyle. Pyle dabbled in sports promotion, earning him the nickname "Cash and Carry" Pyle. During the 1925 football season, rumors began to circulate that Grange had hired Pyle as his agent and would turn pro.

Grange played that last college game against Ohio State on November 21, leading his team to a 14–9 victory before a standing-room-only crowd of eighty thousand people. The next day, he went to Chicago and signed a contract with the Chicago Bears.

George Halas, coach and part-owner of the Bears, immediately arranged a nineteen-game, coast-to-coast barnstorming tour. Grange was paid a guarantee plus a percentage of the gate. Newspapers speculated he might earn as much as $60,000—about what Babe Ruth got playing baseball for the Yankees.

Grange's signing drew criticism from some quarters of the college football establishment. "Post-graduate" football was seen as an inferior brand to the game played by collegians. Grange was simply being mercenary in helping sell a cheap product. When his college coach asked Grange why he should get paid for playing football, Grange said it was the same as the coach getting paid for his own football job.

The Red Grange Tour lasted sixty-six days. The tour drew so many people that Grange wound up pocketing $100,000, even more than Babe Ruth. And professional football had gained $100,000,000 worth of publicity.

Fresh from their triumph, in 1926 Grange and Pyle tried to start their own pro football league. That venture failed, and Grange returned to the Bears. Pyle continued to arrange endorsement deals. Grange also starred in two feature films and a movie serial.

Grange retired from football after the 1934 season. He served as an assistant coach on the Bears for a few years and then did some broadcasting and mostly sustained a long career of simply being Red Grange. He died in 1991.

The conventional narrative says that Red Grange saved professional football. Some recent historians have disputed that claim, pointing out that the NFL really didn't catch on until the 1950s and the coming of television. Still, George Halas gave Grange credit for keeping the Bears going. And Halas always declared that Grange was the greatest football player he'd ever seen.

In 1975, an interviewer asked Halas how many yards Grange might run up in an NFL season today. "Oh, about 750 or 800," Halas replied.

"That's not so much," the interviewer interrupted.

"Well, you've got to remember," Halas said with a smile. "Today, Red Grange is over seventy years old!"

JOHNNY AND PHIL

At some time in their lives, most Chicago boys dream of playing with the White Sox or the Cubs. Only a very few do grow up to become major leaguers, and even then, they usually wind up with other teams. So let's look at two rare players, one from the Sox and one from the Cubs. Both were natives of Chicago, and both played their entire major-league careers in Chicago uniforms. And both of them were stars.

Johnny Mostil was born in Chicago in 1896 and grew up in Whiting. He started playing semi-pro baseball as a teenager. During the war year of 1918, he played ten games for the White Sox. The war ended, the regulars returned, and Johnny went back to working at Montgomery Ward's and getting in some ball on the side.

Then the "Black Sox" scandal hit. Suddenly, the Sox needed players. Mostil rejoined the team as an outfielder in 1921 and showed superb defensive skills. Writers compared him to the legendary Tris Speaker. Once centerfielder Mostil reportedly managed to catch a fly ball in foul territory, something even Speaker never did.

Mostil became one of the team's most popular players. During his rookie year, his former colleagues at Ward's staged a Johnny Mostil Day at the ballpark. People in Whiting were proud of him. Traffic on the South Shore Line spiked whenever Mostil and the Sox were playing at home.

Mostil twice led the American League in stolen bases. He could hit, too—his batting average was usually over .300, peaking at .328 in 1926. That year, he was runner-up for the league's Most Valuable Player award.

The following March, the Sox gathered for spring training in Shreveport, Arkansas. On the morning of March 9, Mostil tried to commit suicide by slashing his chest and wrists with a razor. The team announced he was suffering

Hometown White Sox star Johnny Mostil. *From Chicago Tribune, January 7, 1921.*

from neuritis and had endured constant headaches and sleepless nights. Insiders whispered that he was actually depressed over a shattered love affair.

Mostil recovered, coming back late in the 1927 season. But he was never the same player, and the Sox released him in 1929. He later managed in the minor leagues and eventually became a Sox scout. Johnny Mostil died at his home in Midlothian in 1970.

Phil Cavaretta was born twenty years after Mostil, in 1916. Unlike Mostil, he made it to the Major Leagues quickly. He was only eighteen, and a few months out of Lane Tech, when the Cubs signed him in 1934. In his first appearance at Wrigley Field, he hit a home run.

Cavaretta became the Cubs' regular first baseman the following year. He developed into a solid left-handed hitter known for his hustling style of play. Injuries plagued him. Separate broken ankles kept him out of action for much of two seasons.

Cavaretta was rejected for World War II service because of a hearing problem. Now, in his late twenties, he hit his playing peak. In 1944, he made the All-Star team for the first time. The next year was Phil Cavaretta's year.

In 1945, Cavaretta hit .355 to win the National League batting championship. He was elected the league's Most Valuable Player and led his team into the World Series. Though the Cubs lost, Phil batted .423 for the seven games.

Cavaretta was named an All-Star twice in the years after the war, showing he was more than a wartime flash. In 1951, he became the Cubs' manager while continuing to play part time. Just before the start of the 1954 season, owner Phil Wrigley fired him. Always honest, Cavaretta had told his boss that the team had no hope of making the first division.

After twenty years with the Cubs, Cavaretta signed with the White Sox as a first baseman and pinch-hitter. He got into 71 games in 1954 and hit .316. That proved to be his last hurrah. The Sox released him early in the 1955 season.

Cavaretta stayed in baseball another two decades, managing in the minor leagues, working as a hitting coach, and doing some scouting. He died in 2010 at the age of ninety-four. At the time of his death, he was the last major leaguer to have played against Babe Ruth.

PART IV

POLITICS AND POLITICOS

THE MAYOR WHO CLEANED UP CHICAGO

Mayor William E. Dever is mostly forgotten now. Yet once upon a time, he was as famous as the president of the United States. And throughout the country, many people said that Chicago's mayor should himself be the next president.

Will Dever was born in a small town outside Boston in 1862, the son of an Irish immigrant tanner. He came to Chicago when he was twenty-five and worked in a Goose Island tannery while studying law at night. After graduation, he set himself up as a storefront lawyer on the West Side.

Dever became active in the social settlement movement and the clean government wing of the Democratic Party. He was elected to the City Council and became Mayor Edward Dunne's floor leader in the fight for municipal ownership of the city transit lines. In 1910, after four terms as an alderman, the party slated him for the Municipal Court, and he won.

Being a judge was a nice job, but it was a political dead end. Then, in 1923, party leaders were looking for a squeaky-clean candidate to run against scandal-ridden Mayor William Hale Thompson. They chose Judge Dever. Seeing the way the wind was blowing, Thompson decided to retire, and Dever wound up winning an easy victory.

The new mayor took office saying that he wanted to be "associated with something big in the history of Chicago." He immediately launched a massive public works program. Dever built bridges, widened streets, straightened the Chicago River, opened Municipal (Midway) Airport, and replaced the decrepit South Water Market with double-decked Wacker Drive. The parks were spruced up, and his school board constructed a record number of schools. All of these projects came in on time and within budget. Not once was there even the hint of scandal.

Dever's greatest challenge was Prohibition. Intoxicating beverages had been banned by constitutional amendment. Though Dever personally thought that Prohibition was a silly law that needed to be repealed, he was an ex-judge and believed that it had to be enforced while it was on the books. Thousands of illegal taverns—called speakeasies—were operating openly within the city. The mayor ordered his police to shut them down.

At first, the crackdown seemed to work. The speakeasies were padlocked. The bootleggers who wholesaled the banned booze disappeared from the streets. Wild West Chicago had been tamed. Journalists from other states, and even from other countries, descended on the city to examine events firsthand. Dever's clean-up made him a national celebrity. More than a few observers declared he would be a formidable candidate for president in the 1924 election.

But the bootleggers had not been conquered. They had simply moved their operations into friendly suburban towns like Cicero, out of Dever's reach. And within the city itself, the mayor's cleanup eventually backfired.

Think of it this way: Dever's strict enforcement was making it more difficult to sell contraband beverage within Chicago. Business was down, so the liquor traders had to market their product more aggressively to keep ahead of competitors and preserve their own profits. Since they were already breaking the law, there was no reason for restraint in their methods. The result was a major gang war, worse than any that had come before.

So the people of Chicago had gotten grand public works, efficient city government—and even more violence in the streets. And they were starting to get thirsty. As Dever's popularity rose nationally, it declined at home.

William Hale Thompson was watching events closely. Seeing that Dever was vulnerable, the ex-mayor jumped into the 1927 race, declaring that he would make Chicago "a wide-open town." Big Bill crushed Dever by a margin of eighty three thousand votes.

The nation was stunned. How could America's best mayor be beaten by a crooked buffoon? Humorist Will Rogers thought he had the answer. "They was

Chicago's reform mayor, William E. Dever. *Author's collection.*

trying to beat [Thompson] with the Better Element vote," Rogers said. "Trouble is, in Chicago there *ain't* much Better Element."

William E. Dever died in 1929. Today, he is remembered with a public school and a water intake crib three miles out in the lake. Perhaps most significantly, he is also remembered as the last Democratic candidate for mayor of Chicago to lose.

REMEMBERING WILLIAM L. DAWSON

South Side congressman William Levi Dawson is another forgotten Chicago politician. Do an internet search on his name, and it's an even bet that you'll find a story about the composer William Levi Dawson. And yet the congressman was once Chicago's most prominent African American politician and a national figure.

Before there was Barack Obama—before there was Harold Washington—there was Bill Dawson.

Dawson was born in 1886 in Albany, Georgia. He worked his way through Fisk University as a porter, earning his bachelor's degree in 1909. Then he worked at various jobs for three more years before moving to Chicago to attend law school.

While Dawson was in law school, the United States entered World War I. He enlisted in the army and rose to the rank of lieutenant. When the war ended, Dawson returned to school, graduating from Northwestern University. He settled in Bronzeville, married, and began a career as a neighborhood lawyer.

Dawson had always been interested in politics. African Americans traditionally supported the Republican Party, the party of Lincoln and emancipation. Dawson's first foray into electoral politics was an unsuccessful run in the 1928 Republican First Congressional District primary. But in 1933, he was elected to the Chicago City Council as alderman from the Second Ward.

Dawson spent six years in the council. While he was there, more and more Black voters began shifting their allegiance to the Democrats. Dawson himself became friends with Chicago's Democratic mayor, Edward J. Kelly. As a result, the Republicans refused to support Dawson in the 1939 aldermanic election, and he lost. But in 1942, with Kelly's backing, he won the Democratic First Congressional District primary and then went on to win the general election

U.S. representative
William L. Dawson.
Author's collection.

There were no other African Americans in the Congress when Dawson entered the House of Representatives in 1943. Two years later, he was joined by New York's Adam Clayton Powell Jr. The two men's political style sharply contrasted. Powell was direct, flamboyant, and not afraid to court controversy. Dawson preferred to work quietly behind the scenes.

When the Eighty-First Congress convened in 1949, Dawson ascended to the chair of the Expenditures in the Executive Department Committee (later renamed the Government Operations Committee). He was the first African American to head a full congressional committee, and political allies arranged a testimonial dinner in his honor. In his usual low-key manner, Dawson downplayed the historic nature of his new role. "I just want to do a good job," he said.

In 1951, Dawson took to the House floor to speak out against the Winstead Amendment. The measure would have allowed draftees to choose segregated military units. "God did not curse me when he made me Black, any more than he cursed you when he made you White," he told his colleagues. The Winstead Amendment was defeated, a signal victory in the long struggle for civil rights.

Dawson had become the country's highest-ranking Black politician. He was named a vice chairman on the Democratic National Committee. Back in Chicago, as a committeeman who could deliver the vote in large numbers, he had a seat at the table in important party affairs. Those who crossed him did so at their peril.

Chicago mayor Martin Kennelly had been conducting raids against gambling and other illegal activities on the South Side. Dawson thought the mayor's actions were racist. Though Dawson agreed to support Kennelly's 1951 reelection campaign, in 1955 he helped swing the party over to Richard J. Daley.

Daley's election in 1955 cemented Dawson's clout. In Washington, he continued to chair Government Operations. In Chicago, he continued as chief dispenser of patronage on the city's South Side. This went on through the 1960s.

Every two years, Dawson won reelection with little bother. But the civil rights movement was entering a new phase. Some in the younger generation were critical of Dawson's style. In 1970, the congressman announced he was stepping down, naming Ralph Metcalfe as his successor. Six days after Metcalfe's election, Dawson died at eighty-four.

In recent years, scholars have begun to look more closely at William L. Dawson's accomplishments. As the congressman himself might have said, "It's about time!"

CROSSTOWN EXPRESSWAY

For a decade or so, the Crosstown Expressway was the most talked-about street in Chicago. And it existed only on paper.

The Crosstown began with Daniel Burnham's 1909 *Plan of Chicago*. Burnham proposed building a "grand circuit road," a circumferential highway that would ease congestion by allowing traffic to bypass the central city. By the 1940s, the Chicago Plan Commission was putting together a proposed system of express highways for the city. The Crosstown was an integral part of its system.

Under the Plan Commission's 1946 blueprint, the Crosstown would link three proposed expressways. Branching off from the Northwest Expressway near Diversey and California Avenues, the highway would run south parallel to California to an interchange with the Southwest Expressway near 35th Street. Along the way, there would also be an interchange with the Congress Expressway on the West Side. The total length of the Crosstown was about seven miles.

In 1958, CTA folded the Crosstown into its own future plans. This particular project involved extending the Milwaukee Avenue 'L' line to a new terminal at O'Hare Airport. Outbound trains would leave the existing elevated structure at its intersection with the Crosstown, just south of Fullerton. The trains would run in the Crosstown's median the half mile to the Northwest Expressway junction, then head out to O'Hare.

Meanwhile, officials were beginning to question the California Avenue routing of the Crosstown. The Edens Expressway along Cicero Avenue was going to be feeding traffic into the Northwest Expressway from the north. It made more sense to simply make the Crosstown a southward extension of the Edens. Though this route would involve more miles of new expressway construction, it would be much better for traffic flow along the Northwest Expressway.

The revised Crosstown plan using the Cicero Avenue routing was announced in 1962. The new expressway would extend twelve miles to a terminal near Midway Airport at 59th Street. When construction was finished, Chicago would have an all-expressway connection between its two airfields.

But that wasn't all. Another proposal called for the Crosstown to swing east once it passed Midway and then continue on to a junction with the Skyway near State and 66th Streets. The exact route of this east–west expressway was still under discussion. But now Daniel Burnham's plan of a great circumferential highway would finally be realized.

Supporters of the Crosstown touted the benefits to Chicago. The expressway would carry an estimated 100,000 vehicles a day. Half of the traffic would be from drivers who wanted to bypass downtown. Perhaps even more important, the other half of the Crosstown's traffic would be drawn off parallel surface streets. Removing 50,000 vehicles from Cicero, Pulaski, 63rd, and the rest would reduce congestion and be an economic boon.

However, some Americans were taking a new look at urban expressways. Building the highways cost too much money. Their construction uprooted homes and businesses. When they were finished, they cleaved neighborhoods into pieces, while increasing noise and pollution. Revolts against new expressways sprang up in Boston, New York, San Francisco, and other

The Crosstown Expressway's originally proposed route, near California and Armitage Avenues. *Author's collection.*

places. Now, during the mid-1960s, Chicago opponents of the Crosstown were beginning to speak up.

Mayor Richard J. Daley was not about to give up on the project. The 1962 revised plan had called for the Crosstown to be an elevated highway over existing freight rail lines. But as opposition to the highway grew, the "stiltway" plan was junked. Various tweaks on the Crosstown design were then put forward.

The most striking version had the highway's northbound and southbound traffic lanes separated, with a four-block gap between them. Public transit would be part of this expanded median, with the bulk of the land given over to warehouses and industrial use. Or maybe there would be high-rise apartment towers at some locations.

Maverick Democrat Dan Walker was elected governor of Illinois in 1972 on a "Stop the Crosstown" platform. That put the brakes on the project. Finally, in 1979, Chicago mayor Jane Byrne killed the Crosstown. The money that had been earmarked for construction was diverted to public transit.

THE GO-GETTER

They say Emperor Augustus found Rome a city of bricks and left it a city of marble. William Butler Ogden did even more for Chicago.

A native of upstate New York, Ogden arrived in Chicago in 1834 to inspect some land his family had bought. He didn't think much of the grubby little village at first. But he quickly sold off part of the property at a nice profit and decided to stay on as a real estate trader. Within a couple of years, he was rich and one of the town's leading citizens.

Chicago was incorporated as a city on March 4, 1837. Now there would be an election for a mayor and city council. The Democrats named Ogden as their mayoral candidate. His opponent was John Harris Kinzie of the Whig Party. Though Kinzie came from a respected pioneer family, Ogden won easily, 489–217.

Ogden's term was ten months. He appointed a board of health, held an election for school inspectors, and ordered the city's first census, which revealed that Chicago had a population of 4,170. Then the national economy collapsed. The infant city ran out of money, and Mayor Ogden had to pay Chicago's bills with scrip—an official IOU. He personally backed the scrip with his own funds.

In Ogden's time, political office was a public service, not a profession. Chicago's first mayor refused to run for reelection. In 1838, he went back to doing what he did best, being a businessman.

During the next decade, Ogden was involved in many things. He designed the first swing bridge over the Chicago River. He dug a channel to straighten out the north branch of the river, creating Goose Island. He bought and sold land. He backed construction of the Illinois and Michigan Canal. Then, in 1848, he embarked on his biggest project yet—Chicago's first railroad.

William B. Ogden. *From Andreas*, History of Chicago, *vol. 1.*

Ogden proposed building a line west from Chicago to the thriving boomtown of Galena, 170 miles away. The idea seemed like a big gamble, and he had a hard time finding investors. He finally peddled stock to farmers along his planned route, convincing them that a railroad would make it easier—and cheaper—to transport their goods to market.

On November 20, with eight miles of track in place, Ogden declared the first stage of the Galena & Chicago Union Railroad open for business. To publicize the event, he invited a group of distinguished citizens on board for free rides. On the way back to the city, two of the passengers spotted a farmer driving a load of wheat behind a pair of oxen. The passengers were merchants. They had the train stopped, bought the wheat and some hides, and hauled in the railroad's first load of freight.

Ogden's publicity stunt had worked. Chicago caught railroad fever. Within a few years, new lines fanned out from the city in all directions. Ogden's pioneer line eventually reached Galena and beyond, becoming the nucleus of the Chicago & North Western system.

Now Ogden became even richer, but that didn't bother the public. He had a reputation for fair dealing, and he was also philanthropic. As one example of his "giving back," he donated the land on which the city's first medical school was built.

During the 1850s, Ogden broke with the Democrats and joined the antislavery Republicans. As a Republican, he was elected to the state senate. Ogden had become acquainted with Abraham Lincoln through business and actively supported him for president.

In 1862, Ogden became president of the new Union Pacific Railroad, which was constructing the world's first transcontinental line. He was in New

York in 1871 when word of the Great Fire reached him. He returned to Chicago to find his mansion and its priceless contents destroyed. Ironically, his brother's nearby home was one of the few buildings that survived.

Ogden was briefly engaged as a young man. He remained a bachelor until shortly before his seventieth birthday, when he married a lady twenty years his junior. According to friends, the couple had been in a relationship for nearly three decades.

William Butler Ogden died in New York in 1877. He is buried in Woodlawn Cemetery in the Bronx.

DA MARE-GUV

Edward Fitzsimmons Dunne is known as the answer to a trivia question—Who is the only person to serve as both mayor of Chicago and governor of Illinois? He's also known for being the father of thirteen children, though Mrs. Dunne should probably be the one celebrated for that.

The future mayor/governor was born in Connecticut in 1853. His father had left Ireland a few years earlier, after one of the unsuccessful revolts against British rule. The family eventually settled in Peoria. Dad Dunne became a successful businessman and was later elected to the state legislature.

Son Edward proved to be a brilliant student. He attended Trinity College in Dublin until financial reverses forced him to drop out. Undaunted, he moved to Chicago in 1877 and enrolled in law school. After graduation, he became active in local Democratic politics.

In 1892, Dunne was elected a Municipal Court judge. He might have spent the next forty years on the bench if it hadn't been for municipal ownership—the idea that city governments should take over and run the privately owned transit systems. MO was a hot issue in the first decades of the twentieth century. Judge Dunne was a true believer in the cause.

He concluded that the best way he could promote MO was by becoming mayor of Chicago. The problem was that Dunne lived in River Forest. But carpetbagging has long been part of American politics, so the judge simply moved his ever-growing family into the city and got ready for the 1905 mayoral sweepstakes.

Incumbent mayor Carter Harrison Jr. had grown unpopular. Dunne basically scared him into retiring. And though Dunne was a reformer, he also looked like a winner and got support from even the most notorious political double-dealers. Hot Stove Jimmy Quinn—so named because it was said he'd steal anything except a hot stove—summed up the prevailing wisdom: "I care nothing for Municipal Ownership. I'm for Judge Dunne. I have a good job in City Hall, and I'd be a fool to oppose him."

Running on an MO platform, Dunne was easily elected. Now he had to govern. And like many politicians, he found that governing was harder than campaigning.

Dunne came into office with an agenda of progressive ideas. He tried to break the long-term leases tying up school board properties. He wanted to double the saloon licensing fee to hire more cops. He wanted open bidding on city contracts, and there were other grand plans. Still, if Chicago were going to become a modern utopia, the city had to get control of its transit system first.

MO was the overriding issue of Dunne's two-year term as mayor. The privately owned transit companies fought him at every turn. A public referendum on a watered-down version of MO was inconclusive. The city council wouldn't go along with the mayor's plan, and he stubbornly tried to block a compromise settlement. The public grew tired of the bickering. They wanted nothing more than better service. When Dunne ran for reelection in 1907, he lost.

At this point, the mayoral term was lengthened to four years. Dunne had to wait until 1911 to try to get his old job back. But in the primary, he was defeated by none other than Carter Harrison Jr., who went on to win the general election.

In spite of his two losses, Dunne was still the darling of the reformers. In 1912, he secured the Democratic nomination for governor. Though Illinois was a Republican state, this was the year of Theodore Roosevelt's Bull Moose campaign. The Republican split swept Dunne into the governor's office.

Once again, Dunne's great ideas ran into grim political reality. His most important act as governor was securing passage of a law giving women the vote in presidential elections, the first state east of the Mississippi to do this. Otherwise, his term in Springfield was mostly treading water. In 1916 he was defeated for reelection.

After leaving office, Dunne became active in the movement for Irish independence. In his later years,

Mayor/Governor Edward F. Dunne. *From* Chicago Daily News Almanac 1913.

he published a five-volume history of the state titled *Illinois, the Heart of the Nation*. He died in 1937. Ten years after his death, Chicago finally achieved municipal ownership with the birth of the Chicago Transit Authority.

CHICAGO INVADES A SUBURB

On October 25, 1899, the residents of the Town of Austin woke up and found they had become part of the City of Chicago. And they didn't like it.

Most of the community of four thousand people was satisfied remaining a separate town. A referendum had been held, and a majority of Austin voters had been against joining Chicago. But it had happened anyway. The whole thing was un-American!

The story begins in 1865, when the Austin subdivision was created along the Chicago & North Western Railway line, seven miles out Lake Street from downtown Chicago. The area was part of Cicero Township. Besides Austin, the township included the settlements of Cicero, Berwyn, and Oak Park.

Austin grew fast. In 1870, the Cicero Township Hall was built in the community at Lake Street and Central Avenue. Everything remained peaceful until 1898, when the Lake Street Elevated Railroad entered the picture.

Lake Street Elevated service ran through Chicago's West Side to a terminal at Laramie Avenue, the city's western border. The company wanted to extend the line one mile to Austin Avenue. Promised the same five-cent fare that Chicago riders enjoyed, the Town of Austin favored the extension. The rest of Cicero Township didn't see any benefit to them in the extension and opposed it. But Austin controlled township government. The extension was approved.

That did it! Berwyn and Oak Park and Cicero were tired of being pushed around by those Austin snobs at Lake and Central. So they hatched a plan to get rid of Austin. They would give it to Chicago.

Austin was a nice upper-middle-class community with an attractive tax base. Chicago politicians were eager to add more territory, and they let it be known they'd be happy to have Austin become the city's Thirty-Fifth Ward. All that was needed was for Cicero Township voters to pass a referendum surrendering Austin to Chicago.

Out in Cicero Township, signatures were quickly gathered, and a referendum was scheduled for April 5, 1899. A few Austin residents favored annexation and spoke out in support of it. However, most of the townspeople wanted to keep things just the way they were.

On referendum day, voters were presented with three proposals. One called for all of Cicero Township to be annexed by Chicago. An alternative choice was for both Austin and Oak Park to be annexed. The third alternative was for just Austin to be joined to Chicago, with the rest of Cicero Township left alone.

As expected, the first two proposals were voted down. Austin voters likewise rejected the third proposal, to join their town to Chicago, by a margin of 372 votes. However, in the other parts of Cicero Township, enough voters favored the proposal to tilt the election. By a township-wide margin of 182 votes, Austin was cut loose from Cicero Township and picked up by Chicago.

The anti-annexation Austin group was furious. "How is it fair that Austin should be joined to Chicago against the wishes of its voters?" an Austin official asked. "How is it fair that Austin receives a five-cent elevated fare when others of Cicero Township do not?" a Berwyn official responded.

Now the anti-annexation Austinites filed appeals. Various legal maneuvers were tried, such as claiming the referendum was illegal because the Township of Cicero's original charter made it an indivisible unit of government. The Superior Court rejected all the appeals. Finally, on October 20, the Illinois Supreme Court weighed in, affirming the lower court. The referendum was legal. Austin was to become part of Chicago.

Austin Town Hall, memorial to the lost cause of 1899. *Photograph by the author.*

October 24, 1899, was the last day for an independent Austin. Cicero Township police were withdrawn, replaced by twenty-one Chicago cops. Five Chicago firemen settled into the Austin firehouse and began playing checkers. No local resistance was encountered.

Though over a century has gone by since annexation, the Austin community still calls its park fieldhouse the town hall. And the 'L' line that started the ruckus now runs all the way through the Village of Oak Park to Harlem Avenue.

WHO'S THE MAYOR HERE?

During the first four decades after incorporation, the City of Chicago held its municipal elections in November, concurrent with federal elections. Then, in 1875, the Chicago City Council moved those municipal elections to April. The reason given was to make sure local issues would be highlighted when voters cast their ballots.

Yet appearances can be deceiving, especially where politics is concerned. The change in the election date was part of a bitter battle for control of the city. Before it was over, Chicago would have two mayors—at the same time.

As 1875 got underway, the incumbent mayor was Harvey D. Colvin. He had been elected to a two-year term in November 1873. Colvin had run under the banner of the Peoples Party, a "wet" offshoot of the Republican Party that opposed the city's Sunday saloon-closing law. Once in office, he made good on his promise by getting the city council to repeal the law.

Unfortunately, Colvin's administration also earned a reputation for corruption. One newspaper said he was packing city offices with "blacklegs, pimps, grogshop loafers, communist lazzaroni, and other political deadbeats." The Citizens Association of Chicago, a local "good government" group, sponsored a referendum to adopt a new city charter. Their idea was to cut Colvin's term short by holding municipal elections in April 1875 instead of the following November.

But Colvin outmaneuvered them. His council majority scheduled the referendum for April 25. When the referendum passed, it was too late to hold municipal elections in April 1875. So under the new law, the next municipal election was pushed back from its original November 1875 date to April 18, 1876. The sitting city council now had five extra months in office.

That wasn't all. Colvin's city council had pointedly excluded the mayor's office from that April 1876 election. Since mayoral elections were supposed to be held in odd-number years, Colvin declared that he was entitled to continue in office through April 1877!

The anti-Colvin forces seethed. As the months passed, their anger grew. On April 11, 1876—one week before the scheduled city council election—they staged a mass meeting at the Exposition Building. The *Tribune* reported that forty thousand people showed up. That figure was probably inflated, but it does capture the fighting mood of the audience.

The keynote address was delivered by former mayor John Wentworth. He noted that exactly fifteen years ago that very day, another mass meeting had been called in response to the Confederate Rebels' attack on Fort Sumter. "The dangers to our country are as imminent now as they were then," Long John thundered. Colvin and his minions aimed at "the destruction of the purity of the ballot-box!"

Thomas Hoyne, onetime city clerk and probate court justice, had announced his availability to be mayor. The meeting endorsed Hoyne's candidacy, cheered him, and then adjourned.

April 18 came. Since there was no mayoral election on the ballot, Hoyne's supporters had to write him in. He received 33,064 votes. Meanwhile, in the city council elections, most of the Colvin supporters were voted out of office.

Mayoral claimant Thomas Hoyne. *From Andreas,* History of Chicago, *vol. 2.*

The new city council took office on May 8. A majority of the council immediately declared that Thomas Hoyne had been elected mayor. The next day, Hoyne was sworn in.

Colvin was not ready to give up. He claimed that he was still mayor. Though the city council and most city departments accepted Hoyne's election, the city comptroller backed Colvin. So did the police department. When Hoyne attempted to take charge of the mayor's office, the cops turned him away.

For twenty-eight days, Chicago had two men calling themselves mayor. Finally, on June 5, the Cook County Circuit Court settled the matter. The court ruled that the April 18 mayoral election was illegal, so Thomas Hoyne had never actually been mayor. However, if the city council wanted to schedule a new mayoral election, the court said that was fine.

That special election was held on July 12. Neither Harvey Colvin nor Thomas Hoyne were candidates. Monroe Heath, a Republican, won a landslide victory with nearly 64 percent of the votes, defeating Democrat Mark Kimball. On July 24, he was sworn in as the twenty-eighth mayor of Chicago.

PART V

ENTERTAINMENT

ROBIN AND THE SEVEN HOODS

In 2019, WGN radio host Justin Kaufmann conducted a poll to select the Ultimate Chicago Movie. Listeners to his program were invited to vote online for the film that best captured the essence of the city. The winner was *The Blues Brothers*, beating out runner-up *Ferris Bueller's Day Off*.

The subject here is what might be called the Wannabe Ultimate Chicago Movie, a film that unashamedly plays to the city's stereotypes. Mix in a bit of Robin Hood and a bit of Snow White, and you have 1964's *Robin and the Seven Hoods*.

Following in the wake of *Ocean's Eleven*, *Sergeants Three*, and *Four for Texas*, *Robin/Seven* is the final installment of the Rat Pack Quadrilogy. The characters and the plots of the films are unconnected. The idea was to present a musical showcase for Frank Sinatra and his pals.

Robin/Seven was directed by veteran pro Gordon Douglas. David R. Schwartz, a TV writer best known for penning forty-four episodes of the *Amos 'N' Andy Show*, did the screenplay. Sinatra's longtime collaborators Sammy Cahn and James Van Heusen provided the music.

The story opens at a birthday party for Chicago's top Prohibition-era mobster, Big Jim Stevens (Edward G. Robinson). In the middle of the celebration, the guests do a twenty-one-gun salute—right at the birthday boy. That takes care of Big Jim.

Guy Gisborne (Peter Falk) is the man behind the killing. Now Gisborne announces he is forming a syndicate of all the city's gangs, with himself as the big boss. Corrupt Sheriff Glick (Robert Foulk) will provide legal protection, in return for 50 percent of the profits.

North Side boss Robbo (Frank Sinatra) was out of town when Big Jim was hit. He wants to remain an independent operator. His associates include John (Dean Martin) and Will (Sammy Davis Jr.). For some reason, there's nobody named Tuck.

A gang war breaks out, Gisborne versus Robbo. Each man wrecks the other man's gambling resort. In the middle of this, Robbo is visited by Big Jim's refined daughter Marian (Barbara Rush). She offers him $50,000 to find and kill her father's killer. Though Robbo is attracted to Marian, he turns down the deal.

Meanwhile, Gisborne has eliminated Sheriff Glick and replaced him with cut-rate Sheriff Potts (Victor Buono). Marian assumes that Glick was behind Daddy's death and that Robbo is behind Glick's "disappearance." She sends Robbo the $50,000. Instead, Robbo gives the money to an orphanage run by Allen A. Dale (Bing Crosby).

Word of Robbo's charity makes him a hero—Chicago's Robin Hood. The kids at the orphanage form a band of Merry Men, complete with green triangular hats. Business at Robbo's new joint booms. So Gisborne and Sheriff Potts frame Robbo for Sheriff Glick's murder. Robbo stands trial and is acquitted. Grateful for his freedom, he sings that Chicago is "my kind of town."

The last twenty minutes of the film provide a final plot twist that might have been anticipated. A new boss takes over the rackets, leaving Robbo and his buddies literally out in the cold.

Robin/Seven is a lightweight film that's not meant to be taken seriously. The reviews were mixed. A few critics did single out Peter Falk's performance as Guy Gisborne and predicted a bright future for the future Lieutenant Columbo.

The musical numbers are the heart of the movie. Sammy Davis Jr. gives a bang-up song and dance tour-de-force with a machine gun in a piece titled "Bang! Bang!" Bing Crosby and company warn about the evils of drink in "Mr. Booze," a rousing gospel-style showstopper. And of course, there's Frank Sinatra's love letter to the Windy City, the Oscar-nominated "My Kind of Town."

Fans of the Rat Pack knew what to expect when they went to see *Robin/Seven*, and they were not disappointed. The film was one of the top grossers of 1964.

Though some of the movie has not aged well by today's standards, it endures as a historical landmark. *Robin and the Seven Hoods* is the last musical feature film made by Bing Crosby—and the last musical feature film made by Frank Sinatra. For those reasons, it's worth a look.

HOUDINI LEARNS A LESSON

Harry Houdini was twenty-four years old when he arrived in Chicago in January 1899. He was trying to make his way in show business and was getting old. Time was passing him by!

He had started out doing card tricks and various magic stunts, including a trunk-switcheroo with his wife, Bess. Those were okay, but they didn't set him apart. Now Houdini had come up with a different angle. He would become the ultimate free man, the man who couldn't be held prisoner by cuffs or shackles or any restraint.

Houdini had made the acquaintance of Chicago police lieutenant Andrew Rohan. On January 4, Rohan arranged for Houdini to demonstrate his escape skills at the Central Police Station. Over two hundred people turned up—beat cops, detectives, high-ranking department officials, miscellaneous curiosity seekers and, of course, reporters.

After "Monsieur Houdini" introduced himself, Rohan clamped a pair of the latest-model cuffs on the performer's hands. Next he put a pair of leg irons on Houdini's ankles. Then, using a second pair of cuffs, Rohan connected the handcuffs to the leg irons, putting Houdini into a stooping position. With that, two detectives picked up Houdini and carried him across the room. They set him down on the floor of an upright cabinet, pulled the curtain shut, and left him to his fate.

Less than a minute later, Houdini emerged smiling from the cabinet, carrying the restraining devices in his hands. For the next hour, other officers tried unsuccessfully to bind him with ropes, cords, and other handcuffs. Houdini then closed his performance with a series of card tricks.

The next day's newspapers reported the story of Houdini's triumph. Now that he had everyone's attention, Houdini announced a public challenge. Local police officers were invited to attend Houdini's performances at Middleton's Clark Street Museum, bringing along whatever cuffs they thought might contain him. Anyone who could lock the "Handcuff King" in cuffs he couldn't open would win a $50 prize—about $1,700 in today's money.

The challenge had the desired effect. Houdini played to packed houses. At each performance, a few hopefuls came forward with cuffs, which he easily removed.

It was more of the same at the January 11 show. Then Sergeant John Waldron of the Evanston police clamped another pair of cuffs on Houdini, and the performer retreated to his curtained cabinet to remove them. Twenty minutes later, Houdini reappeared. He was still wearing the cuffs. Sergeant Waldron had beaten him.

"Sergeant Waldron of Evanston Wins Houdini's $50 Wager." Thus the story was reported in the next day's *Inter Ocean*. According to that report, Waldron had studied Houdini's methods and concluded that Houdini had broken out of handcuffs by manipulating the springs. Waldron had simply replaced the springs and riveted the cuffs into place. "Houdini declared that Waldron's handcuffs were the first he had ever failed to open," the article concluded.

FETTERED AND FREED.

Young Harry Houdini, starting to make his name. *From* Champaign Daily News, *October 24, 1899.*

Houdini felt that the Evanston cop had played unfairly, but that didn't matter. His carefully crafted image of the man who could always escape had been shattered. His career was in ruins. He'd have to take a job in a lock factory or find some other meaningless work. He went to the Clark Street Museum and began packing his things.

The stage manager at the museum, a Mr. Hedges, was surprised that Houdini was giving up so easily. He said that Houdini still had a job, if he wanted it. The sabotaged-handcuff fiasco could have happened to anyone. The whole thing would quickly blow over. But in the future, Houdini should probably examine any handcuffs before he allowed them to be snapped on.

Hedges was correct in his assessment. Houdini's defeat was only a temporary bump in his successful Chicago engagement. After that, he moved on to other cities, challenging anyone to restrain him, carefully checking the devices, and then escaping from any kind of restraint. And of course, this was only the beginning of a career that would eventually make Harry Houdini the world's most famous escape artist.

But it took an Evanston cop to teach him a valuable lesson—in show business, as in life, never take anything for granted.

CALL NORTHSIDE 777

Anybody interested in Chicago history should set aside two hours to watch this 1948 movie. *Call Northside 777* was the first major Hollywood production filmed on the streets of Chicago.

Granted, the style might not be to your taste. The movie is a docudrama, complete with a narrator. There is no background music, no humor, no romantic love story. Parts of it move slowly. The director is Henry Hathaway, a solid professional best known for delivering action-heavy Westerns.

The film opens in 1933. Two men try to rob a speakeasy and wind up killing a policeman named Bundy. A little later, a couple of Polish laborers are arrested. One of them is Frank Wiecek (Richard Conte). The two men are convicted of murder and get ninety-nine years in state prison.

Now we move forward to 1944. Newspaper editor Brian Kelly (Lee J. Cobb) comes across a personal ad. Somebody is offering a $5,000 reward for the real killers of Officer Bundy in the stick-up. That's serious money in 1944—the equivalent of $70,000 today. Time to call in ace reporter P.J. McNeal!

McNeal is played by James Stewart, in one of the first movies he made after *It's a Wonderful Life*. That movie had bombed at the box office. Now Stewart was trying to restart his career by trying grittier roles.

The editor tells McNeal to phone the number in the ad—Northside 777—and find out what's going on. It turns out the ad was placed by Wiecek's aged mother. She'd been working nights as a scrubwoman for ten years, trying to get enough money to clear her son.

McNeal is touched by Mrs. Wiecek's devotion. Though he privately thinks her son really is guilty, he agrees to investigate the case. This is where the location shooting comes in.

The dogged reporter roams all over 1948 Chicago. He pops up out of the subway near Polk Street and wanders around on Honore Street and all through the old Polish neighborhood. We half-expect him to bump into Nelson Algren in a tavern. The most interesting site is the street where Wiecek's mother lives. Her home is just east of Holy Trinity Church, right where the Kennedy Expressway is today.

The more McNeal digs, the more he's convinced Wiecek is innocent. The police still think Wiecek is a cop-killer and resent any attempts to help him. The politicians don't like McNeal's persistence either. In the end, justice is served. Wiecek is set free.

Call Northside 777, McNeal's Chicago. *Author's collection.*

We should mention that technology plays an important part in *Northside*'s plot. McNeal uses a lie detector and a wire photo to help make his case. These devices were considered state-of-the-art in 1948.

Part of the fun in watching an older movie is identifying some of the minor players. E.G. Marshall shows up, as does wrestler-turned-actor Henry Kulky, a familiar face in scores of 1950s TV shows. Betty Garde is fearsome and totally unlikable as the witness who fingers Wiecek. Richard Conte, who plays Frank Wiecek, is today best known for his role as Barzini in *The Godfather*.

Call Northside 777 opened to favorable reviews but mixed box office. The film received a total of zero Oscar nominations. In the years since 1948, its reputation has grown, and many cinema historians consider it a classic.

The movie is based on a true story. On December 9, 1932, Chicago policeman William Lundy was killed during the robbery of a speakeasy at 4312 South Ashland Avenue. Joe Majczek and Ted Marcinkiewicz were given ninety-nine-year sentences for the murder. In 1944, Joe's scrubwoman mother, Tillie, posted the "$5,000 reward" ad in the *Chicago Times*, which led reporter James McGuire to investigate the case. McGuire's work resulted in pardons and monetary compensation for the two men and a Pulitzer Prize for himself. The real killers of Officer Lundy were never found.

There is also a Chicago-style postscript to the movie. Though the screenplay changed her name, the real-life witness against the two M-men sued Twentieth Century-Fox for subjecting her to "humiliation and dishonor." The studio eventually paid her a settlement of $25,000—a full $1,000 more than Joe Majczek received for spending eleven years in prison.

SMELL-O-VISION

Smell-O-Vision. The word sounded like a joke, and it had been used that way in a 1944 Bugs Bunny cartoon. Yet as 1959 clicked over into 1960, Smell-O-Vision was a real thing and big news in Chicago.

The motion picture industry had been answering the challenge of television with various gimmicks, such as 3-D and extra-wide screens. Smell-O-Vision was the latest. It was an attempt to add odors to movies.

Using smells to advance a plot had been tried before. In the nineteenth century, dramatists experimented with different supplemental odors in theaters. Pine needles were used to simulate the smell of a forest. A restaurant scene might be enhanced by bringing freshly cooked food on stage.

The first use of added smell in a movie theater took place in 1916 in Forest City, Pennsylvania. The theater was showing a silent newsreel of the Pasadena Rose Parade, so the proprietor dipped a wad of cotton wool in rose oil and dispersed the smell with an electric fan. In the years following, there were isolated attempts to supplement the action on the screen with perfume, tobacco smoke, and other strong odors.

Hans Laube, a Swiss national, presented a smell-enhanced short titled *Mein Traum* (My Dream) at the 1940 New York World's Fair. At different parts of the film, the projectionist released tar, coconut, peaches, and other odors into the auditorium by pipes under the patrons' seats. Laube called his system Smell-O-Drama. After a small initial buzz, Laube's idea was forgotten.

In 1956, entertainment impresario Mike Todd was putting together his first movie epic, *Around the World in Eighty Days*. He planned to add Laube's smell enhancers to the film but ultimately decided against it. The movie was a blockbuster success anyway. Then, in 1958, Todd was killed in a plane crash.

Mike Todd Jr. had worked with his father on *Around the World*. Early in 1959, the younger Todd announced he'd be making a movie using the Laube process, now renamed Smell-O-Vision. *Scent of Mystery*, a thriller starring Denholm Elliott and Peter Lorre, was filmed that summer in Spain. After production wrapped, Chicago's Cinestage Theater was refitted at a cost of $15,000—about $150,000 in today's money—for a planned world premiere on January 6, 1960.

And then Todd began beating the publicity drums. "First they moved (1895)! Then they talked (1927)! Now they smell (1960)!" read one bit of advertising copy. Another blurb told the public, "If you never smell another motion picture in your life, you must smell *Scent of Mystery!*" Meanwhile, cast members and the production crew gave uncounted interviews on radio, television, and in print media.

Todd went all out for the January 6 premiere. Hollywood celebrities were flown in to add their glamour, most notably his father's widow, Elizabeth Taylor, who had an uncredited cameo in the movie. The public was entranced, too. A travel agency in Rock Island even arranged a two-day bus tour to Chicago and the premiere.

On the big night, searchlights searched the sky and music wafted over Dearborn Street. This was the biggest movie night in the Windy City since Cecil B. DeMille's world premiere of *Northwest Mounted Police* twenty years earlier. Then it was time for *Scent of Mystery*.

During the movie, cues on the soundtrack caused the release of various odors into the theater. Technical problems kept the Smell-O-Vision from working properly in the initial screening. Still, most of the opening-night audience praised this latest advance in moviemaking.

That didn't last. By the time all the kinks in the system were worked out, mixed reviews and poor word-of-mouth killed the movie's chances. Todd's pet project was later rereleased under the title *Holiday in Spain*—without the Smell-O-Vision.

Mike Todd Jr. left the movie business with a total of three films to his credit. Peter Lorre continued with his distinguished career and tried to forget Smell-O-Vision. Denholm Elliott finally recovered from *Scent of Mystery*, going on to play Marcus Brody in two Indiana Jones movies.

In 2015, a restored, scented version of *Scent of Mystery* had a limited run in Los Angeles and two other cities. At this time, there are no plans for another Smell-O-Vision production.

CITIZEN WELLES AT WOODSTOCK

For over 120 years, the Opera House in Woodstock has stood at the southern end of the town square. In 1934, entertainment history was made there. That's when a nineteen-year-old prodigy named Orson Welles scored his first triumph.

Welles had started acting as a student at the nearby Todd School for Boys. After that, he bounced around the theatrical world for a few years. Meanwhile, back at Todd, headmaster Roger Hill was making tentative plans for a summer drama course.

Hill had been Welles's teacher and mentor at Todd School. Now Welles returned to Woodstock, took the course idea, and proceeded to "jazz it up." He proposed a full-scale summer drama festival at the Opera House.

Welles knew all about the old summer-stock barn shows. His vision was for something greater. Each year, music lovers made pilgrimages to Bayreuth and Salzburg in Europe. He wanted to create the same excitement at Woodstock. In Chicago, the Century of Progress world's fair would be entering its second summer. Plenty of fairgoers could be persuaded to make the fifty-mile journey out to the enchanting town. Woodstock would become the summer capital of American theater!

Headmaster Hill signed on. Then Welles went to work.

He secured the "delighted co-operation" of the Woodstock Chamber of Commerce. He imported two noted actors he'd met in Ireland. He recruited prominent Chicagoans for a Friends of the Festival Committee. He threw parties. He charmed reporters. He turned out mountains of publicity.

The festival opened on July 12. Patrons motored in from all over the city and the North Shore, and the press came on a chartered bus. "It is a gala occasion, perhaps the most exciting the little town of Woodstock has ever had," the *Tribune* reported. "The whole town was out to watch the guests assemble in front of the theatre."

The first play was *Trilby*, a once-popular relic of the 1890s. Teenager Welles directed and also played the villain hypnotist, Svengali. His makeup was so realistic that his fellow Todd School alumni didn't recognize him until they read the program. The reviews of the play were mainly positive. And everyone loved the venue.

Trilby ran for two weeks. Next on the bill was *Hamlet*. Rather than play the title character, Welles cast himself as another villain, King Claudius. Here he began to experience the controversy that would dog his entire career.

Welles's performance as Claudius was over the top. Many patrons didn't like it, and one critic said that Welles made the character "look like a decadent Roman emperor after a bad night on the banqueting couch." But as the same reviewer noted, that was the point. "Claudius is the villain in a melodrama, and a completely detestable fellow."

The season closed with *Tsar Paul*. This Russian tragedy had never been staged in America. Again, Welles played a supporting role, a sixty-year-old general. Here he was powerful yet restrained, making the audience forget he wasn't even old enough to vote.

Woodstock Opera House, site of Orson Welles's first triumph. *Photograph by the author.*

The final curtain was lowered on August 19. The venture had been a grand artistic success, though the financial results were mixed. Welles moved on with his career and never staged a second festival in Woodstock. Still, he always remembered the town fondly, from his years at the Todd School and from the magic summer of 1934.

In 1946, Welles was set to direct and star in a thriller called *The Stranger*. He wanted to film on location at the Todd School but was turned down by the studio. Years later, an interviewer asked him about his hometown. "I suppose it's Woodstock, Illinois, if it's anywhere," the Kenosha-born Welles said. "If I think of a home, it's that."

Today, the Woodstock Opera House continues to provide a variety of live entertainment. The big summer event is the annual Mozart festival. The town was also the major location for Bill Murray's movie *Groundhog Day*.

Orson Welles has become a legend. And the legend was born at Woodstock in 1934. Drama critic Claudia Cassidy saw it coming when she wrote: "Perhaps the Festival's chief achievement will be to permit a lot of people to say of Orson Welles, 'I saw him when…'"

M SQUAD

Television came of age in the 1950s. Historians have identified a number of classic "Chicago" TV shows from that era—*Garroway at Large*, *Zoo Parade*, *Studs' Place*, and so on. Often forgotten is *M Squad*.

Unlike those other shows, *M Squad* did not break new ground. It was a cop show set in Chicago, and cop shows were already popular when *M Squad* premiered on the NBC network on September 20, 1957. Los Angeles had *Dragnet*; San Francisco had *The Lineup*. *M Squad* was a thirty-minute drama about an elite unit of Chicago detectives.

Starring in the new series was Lamont Waltman Marvin Jr., better known by his stage name, Lee Marvin. He portrayed Lieutenant Frank Ballinger. Marvin had appeared in supporting roles in *The Caine Mutiny*, *The Wild One*, and other movies. A tough-guy U.S. Marine combat vet, he was perfect as the no-nonsense Ballinger. The other recurring character was Captain Grey, played by Paul Newlan.

Though never explained as such, Ballinger and his colleagues were brought in to solve cases that could not be handled by the regular police. At the same time, there was also no explanation of what the "M" in the squad name stood for. The real Chicago Police Department didn't have anything like an M Squad. The idea was to give the writers a lot of story latitude.

"In a town like Chicago, anything can happen, and usually does," Ballinger muses. As a result, he often goes undercover. He can pose as a furniture salesman or a mob hit man, a jewel thief or an immigrant factory worker, a socialite or a biker thug. Sometimes he arranges to get put in jail. He serves as a bodyguard for a wise guy in witness protection. He tries to find a kidnapped heiress before she dies of exposure or prevent a bomb from blowing up a hospital.

While Ballinger is busy cleaning up Chicago, he runs into a wide assortment of people. Some of these characters are played by actors who'd later become famous. Look carefully, and you'll see Burt Reynolds, Charles Bronson, Angie Dickinson, and others. The episode titled "The Fire Makers" featured a double parlay, with James Coburn and Leonard Nimoy as brothers who operate an arson-for-hire service. (And Nimoy is no Mr. Spock here—he's bug-eyed *crazy*.)

Much of the *M Squad* action was at night, giving it a sinister, hard-edged look. Jazz filled the soundtrack. Some of the background music was composed by a very young John Williams. The later shows opened with a dynamite theme from Count Basie.

The show was not popular with Chicago mayor Richard J. Daley. He refused to provide any help with the series. The usual explanation for his attitude is that one of the scripts had a city cop taking bribes. As a result, nearly all of the filming was done in Hollywood. The producers had to do their Chicago photography on the run.

M Squad—Ballinger's Chicago. *Author's collection.*

"We shoot locations twice a year," Marvin told an interviewer. "No permit, no cooperation, no nothing. They don't want any part of us. We shoot and blow." The most memorable sequence was the opening credit, where Marvin has a night shoot-out on lower Wacker Drive.

And then there are those other brief location shots peppered through nearly every episode. For today's Chicagoan, they are a major selling point of *M Squad*. Here is a chance to see what the city looked like sixty-plus years ago. There are scenes all over Chicago. The camera takes us to Hyde Park, South Chicago Avenue, under the old Ogden Avenue viaduct, along pre-Sandburg Clark Street. The episode "Ghost Town" was shot among buildings being torn down for an expressway. M Squad Headquarters itself was a shuttered police station at Racine Avenue and Superior Street, where the Kennedy Expressway comes through today.

M Squad ran for three seasons, wrapping up in 1960 after 117 episodes. Though the show had strong ratings, Lee Marvin reportedly wanted to give movies another try—and within five years, he was a major above-the-title film star, with an Oscar in hand. In more recent times, Marvin's breakout Chicago detective show was hilariously spoofed by the series *Police Squad*.

HOLD 'EM JOE

Many Chicagoans remember "Spider Dan" Goodwin. He was the acrobat who scaled the outside of the Sears Tower to the top in 1981. In a way, Goodwin was continuing a local tradition that dates from the 1920s and Joe Powers. "Hold 'Em Joe" was a flagpole sitter.

Historians trace flagpole sitting back to ancient Christian monks, who perched on top of pillars as a form of isolation and mortification. The modern version was popularized by an ex-sailor named Alvin "Shipwreck" Kelly. In 1924, Kelly sat atop a pole in Hollywood for thirteen hours to promote a movie. Then other hopefuls began challenging Kelly's record, and Kelly answered the challengers back. By 1927, Kelly was again on top (pun intended) with a sojourn of twelve days.

Now Joe Powers enters the story. He was a twenty-two-year-old Canadian-born sign painter from the Marquette Park neighborhood. In the Loop, the Morrison Hotel had recently completed a forty-six-story tower. Powers convinced the hotel's manager that a new flagpole-sitting record would be great publicity.

At 2:30 p.m. on June 28, Powers began ascending the one-hundred-foot-tall flagstaff on the hotel roof. Earlier, he had constructed a two-foot-wide platform atop the pole. Wearing trousers with extra padding in the seat, he settled himself. The only equipment he carried was a megaphone so he could communicate with the hotel staff and reporters at the base of the pole.

Powers was 637 feet above Madison Street. Time passed, and he amused himself by counting the cars below. For dinner, he ate a club sandwich passed up in a bucket. He told one reporter that the view was wonderful, but he wasn't happy about the ninety-four-degree sunshine.

Chicago newspapers carried news of Powers's stunt. By the second afternoon, crowds had begun to gather on the streets outside the Morrison, straining their eyes for a glimpse of the man on the pole. One entrepreneur rented binoculars to people who wanted to get a better look at Powers. That ended badly when a renter wouldn't get off the glasses when the owner told him to, and the two men got into a fistfight.

Powers sat on! As the wire services spread reports of his quest nationwide, bookies did a brisk business. Each day, the crowds on Madison grew thicker.

On the evening of the eighth day, a thunderstorm hit. Powers sent for a blanket to wrap around himself. A sudden gust of wind slammed him into the pole, knocking out six of his teeth. Still, he would not give up.

"There's one thing that really concerns me," Powers said in a dictated statement. "Some people have the idea that this is just a stunt. It's a serious effort to gather scientific data for the advancement of America's place in flagpole sitting. I'm not doing it for any idea of personal advancement."

Powers sat on! He broke Shipwreck Kelly's record. Finally, a little past six o'clock on the evening of July 15, he came down from his pole. His time was recorded as sixteen days, two hours, and forty-three minutes.

Later that evening, after he'd cleaned up, Powers was honored at a dinner given by the Morrison. A tailor presented him with a new suit, and a dentist took impressions to make some replacement teeth. He posed for pictures with movie star Mary Philbin. Then, after a massage, he retired to a room in the hotel for some sleep.

If Powers did wish his performance would lead to greater things, that didn't happen. His record was soon broken. In 1930, he failed at an attempt to set a new record atop the 2800 North Milwaukee Building. With the country entering the Great Depression, flagpole sitting suddenly seemed silly.

In 1934, Powers snuck onto the roof of the Morrison and attempted to scale "his" flagpole. By then, a new manager was in charge of the hotel, and he had Powers arrested for trespassing. From there, Hold 'Em Joe is lost to history.

Now, as you are no doubt wondering—when a flagpole sitter had to answer the call of nature, the result was deposited in a bucket, which was passed down the pole to be emptied. Presumably, this was a different bucket than the one used for food.

PART VI

LAW AND DISORDER

THE LONE RANGER COMES TO LINCOLNWOOD

The Lone Ranger debuted as a local Detroit radio program in 1933. The Old West's mysterious masked rider for justice soon became a national sensation. In 1949, the show was one of the first to make the transition to the new medium of television.

There was one problem. The actor who voiced the ranger on radio was considered too bulky to make a convincing action hero. The producers set out to find someone who sounded like the radio guy. That opened the door for Clayton Moore.

Moore was a thirty-five-year-old native Chicagoan. A graduate of Hayt Elementary School, he'd dropped out of Senn High School to become a circus acrobat. In 1938, he began working in movies as a stunt man and bit player. By the late 1940s, he was a familiar face in low-budget Hollywood films.

Clayton Moore would make the Lone Ranger role his own. When the producers later tried another actor as the masked man, fans demanded that Moore be brought back. He eventually appeared in 169 TV episodes and two feature films. After the show was canceled in 1957, he continued to travel the country in costume, making personal appearances.

In 1976, Moore was in the middle of another nationwide tour. In mid-June, he was booked for a series of appearances at the Community Family Discount stores in Chicago. He arrived in the city on June 18, intending to check in at the Executive House hotel downtown.

Moore traveled the country in an oversize Dodge van. At the Executive House, he was told that the van was too big for the garage elevators. He offered to park the vehicle on the garage's first floor. The attendant wouldn't allow that either, saying there would be no room for other cars.

Moore phoned his Community Discount sponsors for advice. They found him a room at a suburban hotel with spacious parking, the Hyatt House in Lincolnwood.

At the Hyatt, Moore was concerned he'd have to park the van in an open lot. There seemed to be no alternative, so he found a space just outside his room, under an overhead light. He gave a phone interview to a reporter. Then he went to sleep.

"The next morning I discovered that I had been right to worry," Moore later wrote. "As I carried my suitcase from the hotel to the van, I noticed that something was wrong. The door was dented. It had been forced open. Inside the van, all my belongings were strewn about—all my belongings, that is, that were still there."

Moore had forgotten to set the van's alarm. Making a quick inventory of its contents, he noted that his tape recorder, fishing gear, outboard motor,

Lincolnwood Hyatt, later the Purple Hotel. *Photograph by the author.*

binoculars, and portable heater had not been taken. The Lone Ranger silver bullets were still in their special hiding place. "The thieves must have been surprised during the robbery," he concluded. Otherwise they would have carried the bullets off.

Missing were an authentic badge given to him by the Fresno Police Department and eight replica sheriff's badges. Also gone was an 1833-model Remington revolver that Moore displayed during his performances. The thieves evidently had some familiarity with antiques—the gun was valued at $1,200.

Moore reported the theft to the police. He then strapped on his regular costume guns and went on with the day's appearances. "There will be retribution!" he declared in his best Lone Ranger voice. The stolen items would never be recovered.

"Lone Ranger Robbed!" The story was picked up by the wire services and spread. In the days that followed, journalists and standup comics had a lot of fun with the incident, observing that on TV, the bad guys never got the drop on the masked man. But then, the Lone Ranger had never been to a Chicago suburb.

Clayton Moore continued making appearances as the Lone Ranger into his seventies. A few years before his 1999 death, he published a memoir titled *I Was That Masked Man*. The Lincolnwood Hyatt later became known as the Purple Hotel until it was demolished in 2013. But Clayton Moore's boyhood home still stands at 6254 North Glenwood Avenue in Chicago, a private residence.

THE HOTEL SHERMAN PEACE CONFERENCE

The war has been getting out of hand. So Don Corleone calls for a summit meeting. All the gang bosses sit down together and hammer out a truce.

It's a famous scene in *The Godfather*. But it really did happen—in Chicago in 1926.

During the 1920s, Prohibition was the law of the land. The gangs of Chicago were supplying bootleg booze to thirsty citizens. Warfare developed in the fall of 1924, when the two biggest mobs began squabbling over territorial rights. It was another of those North Side versus South Side conflicts—Dion O'Banion's mostly Irish North Siders against Johnny Torrio's mostly Italian South Siders

The South Siders struck first, assassinating O'Banion in his florist shop. Naturally, the North Siders retaliated. After that, the South Siders re-retaliated. Meanwhile, a number of smaller independent gangs bounced back and forth and around between the two major mobs, adding to the confusion.

By September 1926, Chicago had gotten a national reputation for gang mayhem. The South Side outfit was now being run from suburban Cicero by Al Capone. On September 20, a motorcade of ten cars shot up Capone's headquarters at the Hawthorne Inn hotel. Three weeks later, Hymie Weiss, the mastermind behind the Hawthorne raid, was gunned down in front of Holy Name Cathedral.

Now what? These disturbances were attracting too much attention and could wreck business. The U.S. Senate had begun nosing around, conducting an investigation into the Prohibition law and its effects. Something had to be done to cool things off.

Different sources give different versions of who first broached the idea of a general peace conference. The actual work of organizing the meeting fell to Maxie Eisen, a labor chieftain who had contacts with all the warring factions and was widely respected. Eisen arranged to host the assembly at the Hotel Sherman, in the heart of the Loop across from City Hall.

All the gangs sent representatives, thirty men in all. The list of delegates reads like a who's who of the Chicago underworld—Capone, Tony Lombardo, Bugs Moran, Klondike O'Donnell, Schemer Drucci, to name a few. Weapons were checked at the door. The opening session was scheduled for the morning of October 21.

Nobody tried to keep the meeting secret. The newspapers published reports on the conference, and a police detective attended as a neutral observer. The general tone was set by Maxie Eisen, who told the delegates, "Let's give each other a break. We're a bunch of saps, killing each other this way and giving the cops a laugh."

Everyone agreed. "The dead are dead—long live the living!" one delegate proclaimed. The whole meeting lasted barely two hours.

The result was the Hotel Sherman Treaty. The gangs officially renounced violence as a matter of policy. All standing grievances and feuds were called off. Gangs would refrain from trying to stir up trouble among other factions. The head of each gang would be responsible for punishing his own people. Each group would operate only within its designated boundaries.

The conference adjourned. The delegates then moved on to a nearby café to celebrate their rediscovered amity. There was much laughter and good fellowship.

Hotel Sherman, fifty years after the Peace Conference. *Photograph by the author.*

As usual, Capone made himself readily available to the press. He was pleased with the peace he had helped make. "Now for the first time in two years I will sleep without a gun under my pillow," he said. "I believe it's a peace to stay. I know I won't break it, and I don't think they will."

The reason for Capone's pacifism was logical. "I have a wife and a child whom I love," he admitted. "These other fellows have wives and sweethearts, too. There's plenty of room for all of us."

"Gangsters Sign Peace Treaty in Chicago Loop" the headline read, as the Associated Press dispatch told the country the big news. The immediate, unexpected result was that the city's unsavory image was actually reinforced. Only in Chicago would gangsters hold a press conference to announce their territorial agreements.

As it happened, the gangland truce lasted less than a year. But then, have the diplomats of nations done much better in negotiating peace?

THE IVA BARNES CASE

In 1916, Iva Barnes was a thirty-two-year-old housewife. She lived with her wealthy husband, James, in an apartment at 356 East 58th Street, across from Washington Park. On the evening of September 5, James was found lying dead in the park. He'd been shot in the head three times.

Suspicion immediately fell on Iva. The next morning, she confessed to the killing. And one day later, after lawyering up, she withdrew her confession.

The couple's trouble had started in June. Iva was sitting in the park, sewing, when her pet parrot suddenly became excited and flew up into a tree. Ray Shelhammer, a young bartender who lived in the neighborhood, happened to be passing by. He climbed up the tree and retrieved the parrot. He then walked Iva back to her apartment so he could wash his hands.

What exactly happened there depended on whether Iva or Ray was telling the story. The unambiguous fact is that James Barnes arrived home to find Iva and Ray together. After Ray hurriedly left the premises, James told Iva that their marriage was over. The next day, he moved out.

Iva said that Ray had tried to "force his attentions" on her. Trying to save her marriage, Iva then asked Ray to admit his guilt to James—at least, that's what Ray claimed. In August, Iva did file assault charges against Ray, but the case was dismissed.

So on September 5, the day before James was to file for divorce, Iva met with him for a final attempt at reconciliation. But when they walked in the park, James became abusive. He started swearing, hitting, and kicking her. During their struggle, the gun that Iva carried for protection went off.

On September 11, the grand jury indicted Iva Barnes for the murder of her husband. She was later released from jail on $25,000 bond, pending trial.

Now the case began to take on a larger significance. Elizabeth Hoffman, secretary of the Woman's Bar Association, used the opportunity to urge that more female lawyers be hired in the court system. She asserted that male prosecutors were often too lenient on male defendants. Hoffman also said that she would like to help defend Iva Barnes. "I should offer my servicers free to her defense if a woman were to prosecute her at this time," she told reporters.

Meanwhile, other women were looking at the matter from a different angle. A group of social workers and female lawyers were lobbying States Attorney Maclay Hoyne to appoint a female prosecutor in the Iva Barnes case. They suggested that Agnes McHugh be given the assignment.

Iva Barnes. *Author's collection.*

"A male jury will not convict a woman murderer in this country," McHugh said. "I think this leniency may be traced to the chivalry latent in any man. The jurors see two or three big, strong men sitting at the prosecutor's table and subconsciously think that these fierce prosecutors are attacking the frail, pretty woman in the prisoner's chair. Their instinct is to defend her."

Journalist Honor Fanning followed up on McHugh's remarks. Fanning noted that in the previous nine years, twenty Chicago women had been acquitted of murdering their husbands or lovers. She called it "that unique Chicago pastime—the killing of husbands without paying a penalty."

In the end, States Attorney Hoyne declined to appoint a female prosecutor. The trial began on December 7. On December 21, Iva Barnes took the stand in her own defense.

Frequently sobbing, Iva told of a gloomy marriage to a cold, brutish man who was frequently drunk and sometimes beat her but whom she still loved. She repeated her account of James Barnes's death. From that point on, her memory was hazy. She could not recall her confession. "I don't remember what I said," she testified. "I was thinking only of Jim."

The jury retired the next day. After three hours' deliberation, they found Iva Barnes not guilty.

Outside the courtroom, Iva declared that she would never again marry and would devote her life to the poor as a nurse. For his part, States Attorney Hoyne was not surprised by the trial's outcome. "Cook County juries will not convict a woman of murder," he said. "We shall continue trying them, whether juries convict or not."

PAUL HARVEY GETS BUSTED

Paul Harvey had a long, distinguished career as a radio news broadcaster. At its peak, his commentary program was heard on more than 1,200 stations, with an estimated audience of over twenty million listeners. His weekly column appeared in three hundred newspapers. Yet one mistake nearly derailed that career before it got rolling.

In February 1951, Harvey was thirty-two years old. He'd recently begun broadcasting a daily program out of the Chicago office of the ABC radio network. Now he was contacted by a guard at the Argonne National Laboratory, the top-secret nuclear facility located in DuPage County west of the city. The guard told Harvey that the security at Argonne was a joke.

The Korean War was on. Atomic spies were in the news. Harvey decided to see for himself whether Argonne's security really was lax.

Shortly after midnight on February 6, Harvey drove out to the lab in his car. With him were his original contact and another guard. Parking the car just outside the grounds, Harvey began scaling the ten-foot-high fence. His companions remained behind.

Harvey had just come down inside the fence when he spotted a guard. He began to run away. The guard ordered him to halt. Harvey stopped, stumbled, and fell. When he got up, he was placed under arrest. Meanwhile, the two whistle-blowers outside the fence took off.

Harvey was taken to Chicago FBI headquarters for questioning. Because his driver's license was in his birth name—Paul Aurandt—at first it was thought that this intruder might be an atomic spy himself. When his identity as a newscaster was established, Harvey was released.

After his release, Harvey declined to comment directly on his Argonne visit. He did say that he had "been working in cooperation and conjunction with the investigating divisions of several government departments" for several months. Other than that, he could say nothing further.

The FBI immediately issued a statement denying that it was one of the agencies Harvey had claimed to be working with. Then Congressman Fred Busbey weighed in. "I am one of the persons in Washington who have worked with Paul Harvey on certain phases of an investigation of our nation's security," the Illinois Republican said. Busbey added that Harvey would remain silent on the details of the ongoing investigation, "even to the extent of placing his reputation in jeopardy."

Merlin W. Griffith, an official of the Argonne Guards Union, also came to Harvey's defense. He praised Harvey for exposing "flaws" in security at the facility. "It would be easy for any person or persons that meant to sabotage this great project, to do a good job of it," Griffith said.

The FBI determined that Harvey had not broken any federal laws and dropped the matter. However, on March 15, the U.S. attorney's office announced plans to seek an indictment. The charges involved "conspiracy to obtain information on national security and transmit it to the public."

Harvey had told conflicting stories when questioned. Papers found in his car suggested that he'd sneaked into Argonne to prepare a sensational radio exposé. The motives of the whistle-blower guards were also open to question. The union was negotiating a contract renewal, and anything that might make management look bad would help the union's cause.

On March 21, Harvey appeared before the grand jury. His testimony was not made public. But probably the worst charge that could be leveled against him was that he'd let his enthusiasm get the better of his judgment—a not uncommon fault of young journalists. The grand jury refused to indict. On April 4, Harvey was cleared of all charges. "It's still the land of the free, and I am extremely grateful," he said in response.

Harvey's critics claimed he had gotten off easy, courtesy of FBI chief J. Edgar Hoover. His supporters said that Harvey had been harassed by the U.S. attorney on orders from the Truman White House. Realizing that he might have wound up in prison—or shot—Harvey promised network executives that he'd be more careful in his pursuit of stories.

Paul Harvey received the Presidential Medal of Freedom in 2005. He died in 2009.

THE 'L' SMOKING WAR

In 1909, the Chicago elevated railroad system was operated by four separate companies. Each of them provided a smoking car on their trains. Since over half of adult men smoked at least one cigar a day, that was considered good business. So it came as a shock when the Chicago & Oak Park Elevated Railroad—the Lake Street 'L'—announced that the smoking cars would be discontinued on November 1.

Clarence A. Knight was president of the C&OP. In 1898, he had been the first to add a smoking car to his trains. But Knight had recently returned from a trip to London and noted that the subways there did not have smoking cars. Neither did the subways and elevateds in New York City.

"It's a question of operation, as well as of health, safety, and comfort," Knight declared. His company ran four-car trains during the morning and evening commutes. But for most of the day, the trains had only two cars. One of the two cars was the smoker. Female passengers preferred to ride in the nonsmoking car. As a result, Knight said, "the smoking car never is filled, while frequently the other contains women hanging on straps."

Knight told reporters that he hoped other transit companies would follow his lead. That was wishful thinking. The Chicago Railways remained silent on the idea of banning smoking. The South Side Elevated Railroad stated it had no plans to bring up the subject.

The Metropolitan Elevated was blunter. "Our traveling public wouldn't like it," the company president said. "We have opposed the abolition of smokers consistently, and I don't believe the time has arrived to alter our attitude." Then he added, "We shall watch Mr. Knight's experiences with interest."

Nothing much happened the first few days. The smokers went on smoking, and the conductors looked the other way. That changed on November 5.

During the evening rush hour, security guards on an outbound train from the Loop confronted two Oak Park men who were smoking. The smokers refused to stop. An argument ensued, and about twenty other passengers got into it, defending the smokers. The guards were finally able to hustle the two

THE SPIRIT OF THE SUBURBS.

"Give Me Nicotine or Give Me Death!" *From* Chicago Inter Ocean, *November 11, 1909.*

smokers off the train at the 44th Avenue (Kostner) station and turn the men over to Chicago police.

Now it was war! On November 8, a meeting to protest the smoking ban was called in Oak Park. More than five hundred people showed up, nearly all of them men. They filled the Village Engine House and spilled over onto Lombard Avenue. The windows were left open so that people on the outside could follow the proceedings—and so that the tobacco smoke could be cleared out of the building.

"King Knight" was roundly denounced for his antismoking decree. One speaker said that the C&OP president was trying to distract attention from his refusal to elevate his 'L' tracks in Austin and Oak Park. The president of the Oak Park Women's Club called for a return of the smoking car, since now ladies were being forced to ride with "intoxicated men." Tobacco-friendly politicians from both Oak Park and Chicago threatened to revoke the 'L' franchise. A citizens' committee was formed to defend the civil right of nicotine enjoyment. Then the meeting broke up, with those who came by 'L' happily smoking on their way home.

A few weeks later, the Chicago City Council held hearings on the smoking question. The aldermen heard George Plummer of the smoking group offer to settle the dispute man-to-man. "I am willing to get into the middle of a ring, fight it out with Knight, and abide by the decision," he said. No doubt Plummer thought his audience was sympathetic. Chicago aldermen routinely violated their own "no smoking" rule during council sessions.

But the smokers were fighting a losing battle. More and more of them were being arrested, tried, and found guilty. Though the fines were not steep—the equivalent of about thirty dollars in today's money—the public became convinced that officials took the law seriously. Smoking violations dropped sharply.

Over time, the other transit companies followed the C&OP's lead. By 1918, all Chicago 'L' trains had gone smokeless.

THE CHICAGO CONSPIRACY

Sixty suspicious-looking men had arrived in Chicago. They carried no baggage. They wore odd clothing, kept to themselves, and spoke with strange accents. Our security forces had been notified of their presence. The strangers were being closely watched. They might be terrorists!

That was the front-page story in the *Tribune*—on November 6, 1864. The time of the Civil War.

The strangers had come into town from downstate on the Illinois Central Railroad. Though they said little, their speech identified them as Southerners. Adding to the mystery was their clothing. Most of them wore butternut-colored shirts or pants similar to Confederate army uniforms.

Camp Douglas was located on the city's South Side, at Cottage Grove Avenue and 31st Street. Originally built as a military training post, it had been converted into a prison for captured Confederate soldiers. Within the past week, 750 new prisoners had been brought under guard to the camp. Now there were close to 12,000 men interned there.

Chicago was loyal to the Union cause. Yet since the summer, rumors had spread through the city that Rebel sympathizers were planning to storm the prison and free the inmates. Now that was going to happen. Why else were those sixty strangers in the city? They were part of the plot. Tuesday was November 8, Election Day. The conspirators would use the confusion of the day to carry out their nefarious scheme!

That was the news on Sunday. Early on Monday morning, military authorities and local police carried out simultaneous raids throughout the city, arresting 150 suspected plotters. Some of them confessed. The scope of the "Chicago Conspiracy" then became clear.

On that very Monday evening—the day before Election Day—an armed force of four hundred men was set to attack Camp Douglas from two sides. The prisoners had already been informed of the coming assault and would stage their own uprising at the same time. With the camp taken, the liberated prisoners would be given weapons for the next stage of the plan.

Now armed, the force of twelve-thousand-plus Rebel warriors would march into downtown Chicago. Seizing the courthouse as a base of operations, on Election Day they would fan out, take charge of the polling places and make sure that only votes for the "Peace Democrat" McClellan were registered. They would rob the banks for gold and the stores for supplies. The homes of prominent pro-Union Chicagoans were also targeted for robbery. Then the Rebels would set fire to the city and march away.

But this was only part of their horrid agenda. Now the freed Rebels would be a guerrilla army operating behind the lines, in Union territory. Illinois had three more prison camps. Rallying local antiwar groups to their cause, the conspirators' new army would attack the other camps and free more men. The goal was to form a Northwest Confederacy in Illinois and the surrounding states. Then President Lincoln would be forced to make peace.

Fortunately, the scheme had been thwarted. Election Day went on without a hitch, and Lincoln was reelected. In the months that followed, new facts about the conspiracy came out.

The original plan had been to attack Camp Douglas on July 24. That idea was abandoned for fear Federal authorities had sniffed out the plot. Then the attack on the camp was set for August 29, the same day escaped Rebel

Camp Douglas in 1864. *Author's collection.*

soldiers were to launch a raid from Canada. The Democratic National Convention would also be in session in Chicago at that time, which would offer the conspirators some cover. The August 29 date was also abandoned when the organizers were unable to gather enough recruits to join them. By the time the attack was finally ready to launch in November, informants had already infiltrated the plot.

A military court eventually put eight conspirators on trial. Three men were found guilty of various offenses and given prison sentences. One of these men later escaped. The other two were pardoned by Lincoln's successor, Andrew Johnson.

Some recent historians have asserted that the Chicago Conspiracy never had a chance of success and was blown out of proportion for political reasons.

THE GREAT TRAIN ROBBERY

Most stories about Chicago crime in the 1920s deal with Prohibition-era bootleggers and their gang wars. This book has a few of those tales. But the biggest local crime of the roaring decade took place in a suburb and had nothing to do with booze or the usual cast of characters.

The Chicago, Milwaukee, and St. Paul Railroad's train #57 left Union Station at 9:00 p.m. on June 12, 1924. The fast-mail train had eleven cars and carried no passengers. It did carry cash, jewelry, and securities valued at $2 million—about $35 million in today's money.

A little over an hour into its trip, train #57 had just passed Lake Forest, about forty miles up from Union Station. Then two stowaways climbed over the coal tender and dropped into the engineer's cabin. At gunpoint, the two men forced the engineer to stop at a crossing near the unincorporated village of Rondout.

When the train stopped, four more armed men appeared. Two of them were dressed as railroad workers. Alongside the track, four Cadillacs were parked, the headlights aimed at the train to provide illumination for the next part of the plan.

In the train's third car, eighteen clerks had been busy sorting mail. One of them looked outside and immediately sized up the situation. "It's a holdup!" he shouted. With that, the crew shut and locked the car's doors.

The bandits were prepared for that. They shot out the windows of the mail car and then tossed in a homemade tear-gas bomb. Within minutes, the coughing crew had exited their sanctuary and were lined up. While two of the bandits guarded the train crew, another two put on gas masks and went into the car for the loot. The plan was running smoothly.

Suddenly, one of the bandits spotted a man running toward him. He fired four shots, and the man fell. When the shooter went over to check on his victim, he realized that he'd shot one of his own men.

Meanwhile, his companions went on with their work. They emptied a total of sixty-four mail bags, piling them into the four Cadillacs, then loaded their wounded colleague into one of the cars. Firing a round of rifle shots into the air to discourage pursuit, they drove off into the night. The whole operation had taken twenty-five minutes.

Once it was clear the bandits had gone, one of the mail clerks phoned in the news to his headquarters. A police posse was soon on the trail of the fleeing perps. By dawn, a dozen different squads were combing northern Illinois.

In Chicago, police rounded up the usual suspects. North Side mob boss Dion O'Banion and his associates told their interrogators they had nothing to do with the Rondout robbery.

Rondout Crossing, site of America's last great train robbery. *Photograph by the author.*

While this was going on, an underworld informant called in a tip that a certain sketchy doctor had been treating a wounded man in a house at 53 North Washtenaw Avenue in Chicago. The cops went to the address and found that the wounded man had $1,500 of new currency in his possession. The man, who said his name was John Wayne, was immediately transferred to the House of Corrections hospital.

Now the case began to break. The wounded John Wayne turned out to be Willie Newton, one of a gang of four brothers who'd specialized in small-time train robberies in their native Texas. They'd been recruited by James Maloney, a Chicago political fixer. Maloney had also provided the four Newtons with two accomplices. A trusted postal inspector named William J. Fahy had provided the inside information to pull off the heist.

By August, the eight men were all in custody. The six active train robbers pleaded guilty and received short sentences. Maloney and Fahy, the two "civilian" masterminds, stood trial, were found guilty, and were each sentenced to twenty-five years in prison.

Except for $150,000, all the loot was eventually recovered. By 1938 the eight guilty men were all free.

The events at Rondout are featured in the 1988 film *The Newton Boys*. Today, a historical marker at the Rockland Road Metra crossing commemorates the site of what is still America's greatest train robbery.

PART VII

CELEBRITIES

AMELIA EARHART'S CHICAGO YEAR

Amelia Earhart was born in Kansas in 1897. By the time she disappeared on a flight over the Pacific Ocean in 1937, she had become a record-setting, world-famous aviator. Along the way, she spent a year in Chicago.

Amelia's father, Edwin, was a lawyer whose fondness for alcohol impacted his career and family life. In the summer of 1914, her mother, Amy, was near a nervous breakdown. Amy's Chicago friends, the Shedds, offered to take in her and the two Earhart daughters while Edwin got his act together. That September, the three women arrived at the Shedd home in the Beverly neighborhood.

Amelia was preparing to enter her senior year of high school. The plan was for her to attend nearby Morgan Park High School with one of the Shedd daughters. After getting a look at the school, Amelia balked. The chemistry lab there was "just like a kitchen sink."

Hyde Park High School, near the University of Chicago, had the reputation as the best public high school in the city. Trouble was, Chicago's public schools were neighborhood schools, and the Shedd house was over eight miles away. If Amelia wanted to attend Hyde Park, she'd have to move into its district. According to the way the story is usually told, the three Earhart women were forced to rent lodgings near the school. In September 1914, Amelia enrolled at Hyde Park as a senior in the class of 1915.

After all the trouble Amelia took to get into Hyde Park, she made little use of its facilities. At her other schools, she had always been friendly and active. Now she made no friends. She joined no extracurricular activities. She went to class and then went home immediately at the dismissal bell.

Amelia Earhart graduated from Hyde Park High School in June 1915. The school yearbook has her photo, but no activities or other special citations are listed. She did not attend her graduation ceremony and didn't even bother to pick up her diploma. Though she said that she planned to enter Bryn Mawr College, instead she enrolled at the Ogontz School, a finishing school in Pennsylvania.

In 1928, after she'd become a celebrity, Amelia Earhart returned to Chicago. During her stay, she visited Hyde Park High School. Reminiscing about her year there, she said the thing she recalled most vividly was that her German teacher could never seem to understand her accent in German.

Determining where Amelia lived in Chicago is not an easy task. Contemporary city directories and telephone books do not list her mother.

Amelia Earhart with some Chicago admirers, 1928. *Courtesy of Union League Club of Chicago.*

Her high school—now known as Hyde Park Career Academy—no longer has any of the materials she used to register.

In a 1932 *Chicago Tribune* article, Mrs. Shedd recalled the year the Earhart women lived with her. She said that Amelia—whom she called "Millie"—was then attending Hyde Park High School. At that time, the Shedds were living in their old home, located at 9600 South Prospect Avenue.

So we are left with an intriguing mystery. Did Amelia Earhart take lodging near Hyde Park High School just long enough to be admitted? Once in the school, did she abandon that lodging and return to live in the Shedd home on Prospect Avenue? With a forty-five-minute commute using two streetcar lines, that might explain why she never bothered to stay around for after-school activities.

Of course, this is only speculation. Without concrete proof to the contrary, we must conclude that Amelia's mother was willing to spend the extra money for living quarters near her daughter's high school of choice. Perhaps someday we will be able to determine where Amelia lived while going to class.

Meanwhile, we do know that Amelia Earhart did live at 9600 South Prospect Avenue for at least some of her time in Chicago. Today, the old Shedd home at that address is long gone, replaced by a house dating from the 1930s. So if we cannot point to the actual "Amelia Earhart Chicago Home," perhaps the city can put up a Marker of Distinction on the property.

THE WRIGLEY HIMSELF

The Wrigley Building. The Wrigley Mansion. Wrigley Field.

Three of Chicago's most famous landmarks are named Wrigley. That brings up the question, who was Wrigley?

He was born William Wrigley Jr. in Philadelphia in 1861. His family made soap. Before he was out of short pants, young Will was out on the streets of the city, a basket under his arm, hawking the virtues of Wrigley's Scouring Soap. At thirteen, his father gave him a horse and wagon, and the kid went out on the road. He ranged through the small towns of several eastern states as a wholesaler for the family business.

In 1891, Will Wrigley moved to the new wonder city of the west, Chicago. He was thirty years old, had thirty-two dollars, and decided it was time to run his own business. He began by selling Dad's scouring soap to merchants.

"Everybody likes something for nothing," Wrigley believed. So along with each can of soap he sold, he included some baking powder as a bonus. The baking powder soon proved more popular than the soap. Quickly changing course, Wrigley made baking powder his primary product.

Now he needed a new bonus item to go with the baking powder. Wrigley began giving away two sticks of chewing gum with each box of baking powder. Once again, the bonus became more popular than the original product. So much for baking powder. Wrigley started making gum. He gave his new product a catchy name: Juicy Fruit.

In the 1890s, chewing gum was just catching on. Wrigley had many competitors, but he was a born marketer. "[William Wrigley] was the last of the super-salesmen," Bill Veeck later wrote. "He was a well-upholstered, jovial man who liked people and knew what made them tick." Wrigley enjoyed his work, saying that nothing

Wrigley chewing gum ad. *From Cook County Herald, November 3, 1916.*

great was ever done without enthusiasm. In the early years, he did most of the selling himself. Even when the company became a success, he never quit pushing forward. New flavors were always being tried.

Promotion never stopped. When Wrigley moved into a new market, he hired attractive women to walk around passing out free samples. Merchants who sold the most gum were given free gifts—lamps, razors, fishing tackle, cookbooks, whatever.

And he advertised. In 1907, with the country floundering in a financial crisis, Wrigley saw opportunity where others saw danger. He mortgaged everything he had and bought $1.5 million worth of advertising for the cut-rate price of $250,000. The gamble worked. The economy bounced back from the short recession, and the Wrigley brand was visible everywhere.

In 1911, Wrigley moved into a fifteen-thousand-square-foot mansion at 2466 North Lakeview Avenue, overlooking Lincoln Park. By then, millions of people were chewing his gum. If you asked them why, they probably couldn't have explained it. Yet the simple little item had made William Wrigley one of the richest men in America.

Now he began branching out into other fields. One of his projects was Santa Catalina Island, off the Southern California coast, which he made into a renowned resort. With his nose for publicity, Wrigley decided his gum company needed a headquarters building that people would talk about. In 1921, he bought a site next to the new Michigan Avenue Bridge and erected the terra-cotta wedding cake Chicagoans know so well. It was the first major office building on what was to become the Magnificent Mile.

And the Cubs! All his life, Wrigley had been a baseball fan. When he got a chance to buy stock in the team in 1916, he jumped at it. A few years later, he had the controlling interest. He renamed the ballpark Wrigley Field, spruced it up, and added an upper deck—the vines came later. He also spent money on the finest players available. The Cubs won the National League pennant in 1929 and set a major-league attendance record.

As Wrigley grew older, he devoted most of his time to his western operations, turning the gum company and the baseball team over to others. His last business venture was the Arizona Biltmore Hotel in Phoenix.

William Wrigley Jr. died in 1932. If you seek his monument, there are some dandy ones.

THE CHICAGO COCKTAIL

Sophisticated drinkers know about the Manhattan. Obviously, that cocktail was invented in New York City. Here in Chicago, we can lay claim to devising our own famous mixed drink—the Mickey Finn.

During the 1890s, if you mentioned Mickey Finn, you were likely talking about a character in popular fiction. Mickey was a young Irish boy growing up on a bucolic stretch of the Hudson River, the subject of short stories written by Ernest Jarrold. Jarrold's anthology *Mickey Finn Idylls* was published in 1899.

Around the same time, a bullet-headed, short-tempered little man calling himself Mickey Finn appeared in Chicago. Nobody ever learned if that was his real name or a convenient alias. This Mickey Finn worked his way through the Chicago underworld, at various times operating as a drunk-roller, a burglar, or a fence. For a while, he ran a school for aspiring pickpockets. By 1896, he had enough money to open his own saloon on South State Street's Whiskey Row.

Mickey grandly named his place the Lone Star Saloon and Palm Garden, the garden consisting of a tiny back room with a potted palm plant. The license was in the name of his wife, Kate Roses. A police inspector disdainfully referred to the Lone Star as "a low dive, a hangout for colored and white people of the lowest type."

Business was middling for the first few years. Then Mickey met a Jamaican voodoo doctor named Hall. It was the beginning of a beautiful friendship.

The general Chicago public first became acquainted with the local Mickey Finn and his saloon in December 1903. A special city commission was investigating aldermanic graft. One of Mickey's former barmaids, Gold Tooth Mary Thornton, was called to testify. As the commission members listened intently, she described how her boss operated his saloon.

Gold Tooth Mary said there was a sign at the Lone Star inviting customers to "Try a Mickey Finn Special." If a particular patron looked particularly prosperous, the barmaid would engage him in conversation. She would hint at a rendezvous with many sorts of intriguing possibilities. All the while, she was pushing that Mickey Finn Special.

Finally, the patron would order the Special. A few swigs, and he was knocked out cold. The drink was a mixture of raw alcohol, snuff-soaked water, and a white liquid supplied by the voodoo doctor. The victim was then dragged into a side room, where he was stored until Mickey got around to him.

After closing time, Mickey went to work on the stiff. The victim was stripped naked to make sure nothing valuable escaped attention. Cash, watches, and rings were the usual haul. If the man had nice clothes, Mickey kept those and dressed the victim in rags before dumping him in the alley. For their part, the barmaids got a percentage of Mickey's take—which was just as well, since their customers weren't in any condition to give the ladies a tip.

Mickey had all the angles covered. Some people would drink only beer, so he had another concoction called the "Number Two" that he poured into the beer. According to Mary, her boss had no fear of the police. Mickey boasted that he was in tight with Alderman Kenna and that he always saved the best cigars for the local cops.

This time, friendship and stogies did him no good. Because of all the publicity, city officials revoked Mickey's liquor license.

Mickey thought he had been given a bum deal. Gold Tooth Mary's story didn't make any sense. "I'd lose money feeding dope to the guys that blow in here," he claimed. "I wouldn't get enough money out of their clothes in a year to pay for the dope."

With the Lone Star closed, Mickey left Chicago. He later returned and operated another saloon, though now he was so notorious that he didn't dare try any funny business. After that, Mickey Finn disappeared from history.

But in a way, Mickey did have the last laugh. He reportedly sold his secret formula to a half dozen other saloonkeepers in other cities, and from there it spread throughout America. Today, any kind of knockout drink is called a Mickey Finn.

A QUEEN IN CHICAGO

The death of Britain's Queen Elizabeth II brought back memories of her whirlwind Chicago visit of 1959. But Elizabeth was not the first foreign queen to conquer Chicago. In the fall of 1926, there was Queen Marie of Romania.

Though Marie was not a queen in her own right, she could claim membership in both the British and Russian royal families. Her father was Queen Victoria's second son, Prince Alfred. Her mother was Grand Duchess Maria Alexandrovna, daughter of Czar Alexander II.

Marie was born in England in 1875 and grew up there. After turning down a marriage proposal from the future King George V—Elizabeth II's eventual grandfather—Marie married Crown Prince Ferdinand of Romania in 1893. In 1914, when Ferdinand succeeded to the throne, she became queen consort.

During World War I, Marie worked as a nurse in military hospitals. After the war, she represented Romania at the Paris Peace Conference. With her outgoing personality and refusal to be plugged into traditional female roles, she became the first media celebrity royal. In 1924, she was featured on the cover of *Time* magazine—not with Ferdinand, just her.

Marie talked of visiting the United States for years. In 1926, one of her American friends invited her to the dedication of an art museum in Washington State, and she accepted. That meant a cross-country train journey. And everywhere Marie went, curious crowds turned out to see her. By the time she arrived in Chicago on November 13, she was the biggest news in the country.

Thousands of people turned out at 12th Street Station to see Marie that Saturday afternoon. She was then whisked to City Hall so that Mayor Dever and various other politicians could officially welcome her. That evening, she

Queen Marie's motorcade arrives for another banquet, this one at the Union League Club.
Courtesy of Union League Club of Chicago.

moved to the Drake Hotel for a dinner with some of the city's Important People. Marie smoked a few cigarettes—which showed she was a "liberated" woman—and told stories, joked around, and charmed everybody.

At the dinner, Marie spoke to the city on a radio hookup. "After you have all said such amiable things to me, I hope you shall not be disappointed," she began. She said that every mayor and governor in America believed their city was the best. Then she added, "When my son was in America several years ago, he told me that Chicago was of all places the most beautiful town in America." She was happy that now she would be able to see this for herself.

On Sunday, Marie went on a tour. She visited some sights and had tea with more Important People. At Lincoln Park, she got out of her car and chatted with a group of Romanian women, which put the whole tour behind schedule. That night, there was another banquet.

Monday was more of the same, including a side trip to Gary to see the steel mills. That was followed by a third banquet. Tuesday followed a similar schedule. On Wednesday, Marie left Chicago, after ninety-one busy hours.

There had been a few bumps in her visit. A threatened strike by the musicians' union was negotiated away. Local communists staged a small protest against the royalist pomp. But the great majority of Chicagoans took Marie's visit in stride and seemed to enjoy it.

Queen Marie never came back to Chicago. Her husband died, and their son turned out to be a disaster as king. She died in 1938.

Marie wasn't like other royalty of those days. She seemed down-to-earth, and she knew how to make the right gesture for the right occasion. I'm thinking of the photographers here. When she got to Chicago, Marie very sweetly asked the city press corps not to take flash pictures of her when she was walking down stairs because it blinded her and she was afraid of falling. That was reasonable, so they honored her request.

Now, many Important People would have just let it go at that. Not Marie. At the closing banquet at the Blackstone, she was called on to make a toast. So she stood up, raised her glass, and said, "To the Chicago newspaper photographers!"

That was Queen Marie for you.

JUDGE LANDIS

He might be the most famous judge ever to serve in Chicago. He was certainly the only one named after a mountain.

Kenesaw Mountain Landis was born in small-town Ohio in 1866 and grew up in small-town Indiana. His distinctive name came from the place in Georgia where his father lost a leg in a Civil War battle. Our man Landis never finished high school but managed to earn a law degree—scholastic requirements were a lot looser then. In 1891, he opened a corporate practice in Chicago.

Time marched on. Landis married, started raising a family, made some money, and made some connections in Republican politics. In 1905, President Theodore Roosevelt named him to the federal bench.

The new judge saw himself as a progressive reformer of the Roosevelt school. So when Standard Oil was found guilty of shady practices in his court, Landis hit the company with a $29 million fine—the equivalent of $930 million today. The fine was later tossed out, and the case neatly sums up Landis as a judge. He didn't always follow accepted procedures and was often overruled. At the same time, he made a lot of noise and got a lot of publicity.

He could be completely arbitrary. On one occasion, Landis freed an eighteen-year-old messenger who had stolen $750,000 in bonds, saying the men who trusted a teenager with so much money should be the ones sent to jail. Another time, he couldn't decide on how long a jail term to give a convicted swindler. Glancing up, Landis noticed that the clock read 4:30 p.m. "Court sentences the defendant to four and a half years," he decreed.

In 1920, the country was rocked by the Black Sox scandal. Eight Chicago White Sox baseball players were accused of throwing the 1919 World Series. Club owners had to do something to restore public trust. Bringing in an outsider to clean house seemed the best solution.

Landis was a household name and had a reputation for flinty integrity. Besides, he was a baseball fan. The owners offered him a job as the sport's first commissioner. Landis accepted—on condition that he have total, "czar-like" authority. The owners agreed.

He spent his first years marking his turf. The Sox players had gone on trial in criminal court and been acquitted. Landis banned them from baseball anyway. When Babe Ruth made an unsanctioned exhibition tour, the commissioner gave baseball's biggest star a six-week suspension.

Landis exiled other, lesser-known players. He voided contracts he didn't like. He did many high-handed things. Today, when even the lowest thugs

Commissioner Landis stands his ground against the Black Sox. *From* Literary Digest, *August 20, 1921.*

are conscious of their individual rights, he probably couldn't have gotten away with half the stuff he did.

But the public supported Landis. With his shock of prematurely white hair and granite face, he looked like a prophet come down from the mountain— maybe the mountain called Kenesaw—carrying the Tablets of the Law. The crisis passed. The public again trusted baseball.

And Landis had saved the game. In 1920, when he took over, only one pro sport rivaled baseball in popularity, and that was boxing. Since then, boxing has continued to be plagued by scandals and is now dismissed by most of the public. Without Landis, the same thing might have happened to baseball.

The one thing a modern sports fan seems to know about Landis is that he supposedly kept Black players out of the Major Leagues. This is based on stories later told by two prominent baseball men—after Landis was dead and couldn't refute them. If Landis really was guilty as charged, no smoking gun has yet been found.

He carried baseball through depression and world war. During those years, Landis lived in a suite at the Ambassador East. Early in 1944, he moved out of the hotel and bought a house in Glencoe, near his adult children. That fall, Landis entered St. Luke's Hospital. The public was told he had a severe cold. But he'd also had a heart attack, and his condition soon deteriorated.

He died on November 25, 1944, a few days after his seventy-eighth birthday. Landis was not a religious man, and his body was immediately cremated without ceremony. Today, his ashes rest at Oak Woods Cemetery.

THE COLONEL AND THE BISHOP

In my last book, *Unknown Chicago Tales*, I noted that three of Chicago's four major expressways were named after famous politicians and told the story of the fourth expressway's namesake, Dan Ryan. Now let's look at two men who gave their names to a pair of the city's outlying expressways.

WILLIAM GRANT EDENS was born in 1863 and grew up in Richmond, Indiana. He dropped out of school after sixth grade to work as a messenger. From that start, he moved through a series of jobs. By 1896, Edens was a railroad conductor.

He was also getting involved in Republican politics. Edens made a number of important contacts during the 1896 presidential campaign, most notably future vice president Charles Gates Dawes. In 1905, Dawes secured for him a position with the Central Trust Company in Chicago.

This was around the time that the automobile was starting to become popular. Although Edens didn't own a car—and would never own one—he became convinced that Illinois's future growth and prosperity would depend on a modern transportation network. Now banker Edens became active in lobbying for good roads. He helped organize the Illinois Highway Improvement Association and became its president.

Edens wanted to "pull Illinois out of the mud"—that was the title of the article he wrote for the *Chicago Tribune* on December 22, 1912. In it, he presented a detailed outline of how Illinois should move forward with road building and maintenance. The program would be financed with bonds backed by the state's automobile tax fund.

For the next six years, Edens labored to get the bond issue on the ballot. When it finally passed in November 1918, the United States was deep in World War I and Edens was an army recruiter. For his service, he was given the honorary rank of colonel. He used the title for the rest of his life.

Illinois highway building took off after the bond issue was passed. In the Chicago area, plans were drawn up for an express parkway to replace Skokie Highway. As early as 1941, there were suggestions to name the new "superhighway" for Colonel Edens.

William Grant Edens was present at the opening of the Edens Expressway in 1951. He remained active in civic affairs to the time of his death in 1957.

LOUIS HENRY FORD WAS born in Mississippi in 1914. His family belonged to the Church of God in Christ, a predominantly African American Pentecostal denomination. Early on, Ford decided he wanted to be a minister. While a college student, he regularly preached to the workers in the cotton field near his home.

Ford moved to Chicago in 1933. He started out as a street preacher near 47th and Dearborn. Within two years, he was able to attract enough people to open a brick-and-mortar church in the neighborhood, St. Paul Church of God in Christ.

Ford's congregation grew, and his church prospered. In 1950, he was consecrated a bishop. He became one of the city's first Black pastors to broadcast services on radio. He also became active in politics and in the emerging civil rights movement.

In 1955, Chicago teenager Emmett Till was murdered while visiting relatives in Mississippi. When Till's body was returned to Chicago for burial, Bishop Ford gave the funeral eulogy. "We don't need to send any more missionaries to Africa," he told the mourners. "We need to send them to the backwoods of Mississippi!"

Ford was elected presiding bishop of his church in 1990. He was reelected to a second term in 1994 but died in office in 1995. Chicago mayor Richard M. Daley, a personal friend, spoke at the funeral. One year later, the Calumet Expressway was renamed the Bishop Ford Freeway.

More recently, Louis Henry Ford has been recognized for his role in preservation. In 1941, he purchased the historic Henry B. Clarke House, which was located near his church. Over the next decades, he renovated the house, lived in it for a time, and eventually helped move it to a site in the South Loop. In November 2022, the Chicago City Council officially renamed the building the Clarke-Ford House.

DINGBAT'S FUNERAL

On March 11, 1930, a crowd of twenty thousand people descended on the 5500 block of South Richmond Street in the quiet Southwest Side neighborhood of Gage Park. The focus of their attention was the redbrick bungalow at #5544. They were saying goodbye to the Dingbat.

The Dingbat was the late John Oberta, his nickname derived from a comic strip. He was twenty-nine years old at the time of his death. Oberta had been active in Chicago politics, serving as Thirteenth Ward Republican committeeman and running unsuccessfully for alderman. He'd also operated a florist shop in the neighborhood. But he was best known for his main occupation—gangster.

Oberta was a protégé of Big Tim Murphy, bootlegger and labor racketeer in the Back of the Yards neighborhood. Perhaps as a tribute to his patron—or perhaps to attract voters in the mostly Irish Thirteenth Ward—the Polish Oberta sometimes spelled his name O'Berta. He was smart, affable, and rated one of the best-dressed denizens of the Chicago underworld.

Then, one morning in 1928, Tim Murphy opened his front door and had his head blown off by a shotgun blast. A few months later, Oberta married Big Tim's widow, Florence. After living in the Murphy house for a while, the couple moved in with Oberta's mother on Richmond Street.

Now Dingbat was gone, too. Shortly after seven o'clock on Wednesday evening, March 5, he'd telephoned Florence from his florist shop, saying that he had a couple of business calls to make and would be late coming home. The next call Florence received was from the police.

John Oberta had been found dead in his car on a deserted stretch of Roberts Road, west of the city. He'd been killed by a blow to the back of his head. The two guns he carried with him had not been fired. The bullet-ridden body of his chauffeur/bodyguard lay in a ditch beside the car.

By 1930, the gangster funeral had become a familiar Chicago custom. Dingbat's friends would not scrimp, and Florence was determined to do her part. "I'm giving him the same I gave Tim," she told reporters.

Dingbat's body was brought home to the living room of the Richmond Street house on Sunday. He lay in a $15,000 mahogany coffin with silver handles under a blanket of orchids. A gold crucifix was attached to the upraised lid and a rosary entwined among his fingers. The room was filled with floral tributes.

During the next two days, thousands of people trooped up the steps of the bungalow, paused briefly to view the main attraction, then exited through the rear kitchen. Some of them left Mass cards. A few brushed away a tear. Joe Saltis, Bugs Moran, Spike O'Donnell, and other notorious associates of the deceased were spotted among the mourners. So were various politicians.

The funeral was on Tuesday morning. Two priests of the Polish National Catholic Church conducted a brief service. Then the pallbearers prepared to carry the coffin to the waiting hearse. Out on the street, that crowd of twenty thousand people had gathered.

Site of Dingbat Oberta's 1930 wake. *Photograph by the author.*

"Carry my Johnny out the back way," Dingbat's mother wailed. "Don't let them see him! They didn't care about him!" The pallbearers ignored her and brought Dingbat out the front door.

The coffin was loaded. Then the hearse moved away, followed by four carloads of flowers and a procession two miles long. When the funeral cortege arrived at Holy Sepulchre Cemetery, hundreds more curiosity seekers were there to greet it.

Dingbat was laid to rest a few feet from Big Tim Murphy. There was just enough space between them for another grave. Presumably that spot was reserved for their mutual wife.

Police theorized that onetime associate Frank McErlaine had killed Oberta in revenge for an attempt on McErlaine's life. But the murder of Dingbat Oberta remained officially unsolved. And with the Great Depression fast descending on the country, the gaudy gangland funeral went out of fashion.

At the same time as Dingbat's last rites in Chicago, former president William Howard Taft was being laid to rest at Arlington National Cemetery outside Washington, D.C. Taft's funeral drew half as many people.

PART VIII

THE PASSING PARADE

THUNDER MOUNTAIN

Most of Chicago is as flat as the proverbial pancake. Despite some severe winters, it's not the place you'd expect to find active skiing. Yet there was once a bona fide ski resort located within the city limits.

In the years after the Great Fire of 1871, Chicago became a major center for manufacturing bricks. The ground here is mostly clay. Since the clay was close to the surface, it was easy to mine and thus cheaper to make into bricks. By 1900, Chicago Common brick enjoyed a national reputation. The city had dozens of brick manufacturers and brick dealers.

The Carey family began operating a brick works on the west side of Narragansett Avenue, between Fullerton and Diversey, around this time. The business prospered for many years. Then, for various reasons, brickmaking moved out of Chicago. The Carey Brick Works closed during the early 1960s.

Meanwhile, in the process of digging out clay over the decades, a tall hill fronting on a massive pit was created on the brickyard grounds. A few members of the Carey family were skiers. During the winter, they began practicing their skiing down the slope into the pit.

In January 1967, Chicago was hit by the worst blizzard in its recorded history. Back-to-back storms dumped over three feet of snow on the ground, paralyzing the city for nearly two months. Chicagoans grew bored and surly, with little to do for fun during this enforced lockdown.

That gave Robert Carey an idea. He would convert a family pastime into a new business. In the summer of 1967, Carey announced that the old brickyard on Narragansett would become the site of Chicago's first public ski resort. It would be called Thunder Mountain.

The news was greeted with some skepticism. Still, Carey had a proven record in business and couldn't be counted out. A number of investors signed on. During that summer and into the fall, work went on bringing his vision to reality.

Thunder Mountain opened to the public on January 5, 1968. Two certified ski instructors were on the premises, and rope lifts were in place for access to the summit. Because of the man-made hill and the pit at its bottom, Thunder Mountain claimed the highest vertical drop within hundreds of miles, a full 285 feet. This was no miniature, pretender ski mountain—this was the real thing!

The resort's scheduled hours were 9:30 a.m. to 11:00 p.m., seven days a week. Lift charges were $3.50 during the week, $4.00 on Saturday and Sunday. A parking lot for two hundred cars was available, with a $1.00 charge that could be applied to the lift fee.

In case the weather was bad—that is, no snow and bad for skiing—Thunder Mountain was ready. Five compressors were on hand to feed fifteen snow guns, enough to create a suitable base.

The view northeast from the summit of Thunder Mountain. *Photograph by the author.*

Early patrons marveled at the literal bird's-eye view of Steinmetz High School and other neighborhood landmarks. Look southeast and you could spot the tall buildings in the Loop. Look northwest, and there was O'Hare Airport. And as the ad copy mentioned, Thunder Mountain was the only ski resort that could be reached by CTA bus.

There were grand plans for the future, too. There were going to be three separate ski runs, one each for beginners, intermediates, and experts. A onetime brick kiln was already being converted into an A-shaped chalet. Another five-story chalet with snack bar, lounge, and a complete rental shop was planned for the Diversey Avenue side of the property. There would be a toboggan run and even a 125-unit motel. And perhaps Thunder Mountain might become a four-season resort. Negotiations were underway to purchase a gondola ride from the recently closed Riverview amusement park.

None of these ambitious projects became reality. Thunder Mountain ran into a couple of warm winters and public indifference and closed after two seasons. A shopping plaza called The Brickyard was eventually built on the site.

ICE CREAM AND WHISKEY

There are a million stories in the Windy City. Two of the stranger ones concern food—of a sort.

The first is about a man named Gombien Jean. In December 1891, Jean was a twenty-one-year-old Frenchman who'd recently arrived in the city. He found work as a flunky at the Leland Hotel. On his first day at the new job, he happened to sample some ice cream in the hotel's pantry. That was on Wednesday.

Jean had never tasted ice cream before. He liked it. He *really* liked it! So over the next few days, whenever he got a chance, he ate some more ice cream. If one of the hotel staff needed Jean for some task, they'd find him near the freezer box, happily lapping up his newfound delicacy.

On Sunday around noon, Jean became violently ill. A doctor was called in. Then a second doctor. Both medics concluded that Jean was dying. A police patrol wagon was summoned, and he was rushed to Cook County Hospital. Two hours later, Gombien Jean was dead.

Jean's fellow employees at the Leland Hotel said that the man had eaten so much ice cream that his stomach must have frozen. Afterward, the hotel manager scoffed at this explanation. "I never heard of anyone eating enough ice cream to freeze up his stomach," he said. "The doctor had the man taken away to the hospital. Go see Dr. Henderson."

Henderson was the house physician at a nearby hotel. He had been called in when the Leland's regular physician wasn't immediately located. "I did not examine the sick man," Henderson said. "He was fast approaching death when I saw him." Then Henderson passed the buck to Cook County Hospital.

For their part, the hospital doctors would not immediately comment on the cause of Jean's death. There would have to be a full postmortem examination to determine that.

So reported the *Chicago Tribune* on January 4, 1892. There were no follow-up stories, which suggest that the death-from-ice-cream tale might have been a reporter's prank. However, the following story is fully documented.

The temperature in Chicago was minus-eleven in the early morning hours of February 8, 1951. That's when two policemen found the frozen body in a gangway at 3108 South Vernon Avenue.

The body was that of a young woman. Later, she would be identified as Dorothy Mae Stevens, age twenty-three. Her skin was cold as metal, her eyeballs like crystal, her jaw and legs stiff. The two cops bundled her in blankets and took her to Michael Reese Hospital for a postmortem.

At the hospital, one of the staff heard a groan. Stevens was still alive. Her body temperature had dropped to sixty-four degrees, more than thirty degrees below normal. She was breathing at about four breaths per minute. Her blood pressure read zero.

Nobody had ever survived in such condition, so the doctors weren't sure what to do. They decided to give Stevens blood plasma and a new wonder drug, cortisone. Raising the patient's body temperature too quickly might be dangerous, so Stevens was put in a refrigerated room and gradually thawed out.

By evening, Stevens's body temperature read eighty degrees. She was able to tell her story. After drinking all day, she had passed out. She had been lying in the gangway about eight hours. "It was either God that saved me, or I'm the daughter of Dracula," she said.

Doctors could only speculate why Stevens had not died. Reporters thought it was all the booze she had drunk—the alcohol acted like antifreeze in a car's gas line. That was too simple an explanation for Dr. Harold Laufman, the physician in charge.

"Alcohol may have dilated various blood vessels, making the chilling process much faster," Laufman said. "Fast chilling is known not to be quite so harmful as slow chilling." The doctor conceded that the alcohol probably did lessen the pain Stevens felt.

Stevens had a long, difficult recovery. Complications developed. Both her legs had to be amputated, as well as nine of her fingers. But she survived another twenty-three years, dying in 1974.

Perhaps the lesson to be learned is this—if you like ice cream, in winter you should switch to whiskey.

THE DAY THE SMILES ENDED

On December 4, 1921, the United States government ordered Chicagoans to stop smiling. It said so on the front page of the morning papers.

The saga began in late October, when newspapers in various cities started publishing stories about one Harry M. Phillips. Phillips was a young man in his mid-thirties. He'd gone into Mexico and struck it rich in mining. But when he returned to the United States, he was struck by how sad the people of Los Angeles looked. So he began giving away money.

Phillips said that he had so much money he was tired of looking at it. He wasn't crazy—he just wanted to see people smile. Once upon a time, he'd been a poor newsboy in Chicago. Now he was on his way back home. "Believe me, when I hit Chicago, the home town will know that I have arrived," he said.

On November 1, the *Chicago Tribune* reported that Phillips was due in the city that afternoon. Yet within a few days, he'd become disillusioned. He had planned to give away $25,000. "But every time I try to make people smile, the police appear to stop me," he told a reporter from the *Chicago Herald-Examiner*. "This is a bum town. I'm going to blow back where I came from." After that, nothing more was heard from Harry M. Phillips.

The *Herald-Examiner* wasn't about to let Phillips insult Chicago and its people. The paper would prove that Chicago was the greatest city in the world by carrying out his aborted philanthropy. Each weekday copy of the *Herald-Examiner* would now contain a Smile Coupon with a different serial number. On Sunday, there would be a raffle, with a $1,000 grand prize.

To some cynics, the whole business was now becoming clear. The *Herald-Examiner* was the morning newspaper owned by William Randolph Hearst. The paper was trying to overtake the *Tribune*, and the Phillips story was just the sort of bogus stunt that Hearst often used. This "Harry M. Phillips" was

THEY SMILE! THE CHEER CHECKS WIN!

Some Cheer Checks prize winners. *From* Chicago Tribune, *December 3, 1921.*

probably a Hearst flack who'd been sent on the road to spread a few dollars and set up Chicago for the Smile Coupon program.

The *Herald-Examiner* took pains to assure the public that its motives were not mercenary. Besides being printed in the paper, Smile Coupons were also available for free distribution at groceries, drugstores, movie theaters, and other places. Copies of each day's paper could be examined at public libraries. Still, it was understandable that interested members of the public might want to sign up for home delivery of the paper.

The first drawing took place on November 13. The $1,000 winner was a Sears clerk—and sure enough, she smiled. So the *Herald-Examiner* announced it was putting $25,000 into a pot, to be paid out in $1,000 *daily* raffles.

At first, the *Tribune* took no notice of its rival's raffles. The paper had been taken in by the initial Phillips stories and was probably embarrassed by the fact. But during the early weeks of the Smile campaign, the Hearst paper's circulation jumped 25 percent to 500,000, about the same as the *Tribune.* And on Thanksgiving Day, the *Herald-Examiner* increased its pot to $100,000, with $3,000 in daily prizes.

So now the *Tribune* launched its own giveaway. With Christmas approaching, the paper started printing Cheer Checks. And the *Tribune*'s program would be bigger and better. The World's Greatest Newspaper would be distributing $200,000—$5,000 each day.

Now the whole city was caught up in the frenzy. News dealers reported people buying armloads of papers, ripping out the coupons, and tossing the rest into the street. Fights broke out among customers trying to purchase papers. The daily prizes went to $6,000, then $7,000. The special Sunday drawing reached $20,000.

By December 4, the circulation of each paper was over one million. On that day, both the *Herald-Examiner* and the *Tribune* received telegrams from the postmaster general, asking them to end their Smile raffles. The explanation given was vague.

Both papers used the government message as an excuse to end their competition. From then on, Chicagoans would have to find their own reasons to crack a smile.

THE KANGAROO-HOP AIRLINE

Commercial air travel exploded in the years after World War II. The war had highlighted the use of air power to victory, and now civilians were eager to fly farther and faster than ever before. As it was for railroads, Chicago became a major hub for air travel. By 1950, Midway Airport was the world's busiest airfield.

Midway was on the city's Southwest Side. Taxi and limo service from the Loop was readily available, and the trip out Archer Avenue wasn't bad. But many of the airport's customers lived in North Shore suburbs. Getting to Midway from those towns was a problem.

One way was to take a commuter train into downtown and then catch a cab to the airport. Or you might just head straight down Skokie Highway and Cicero Avenue. In pre-expressway Chicago, either trip could consume over two hours.

Hugh Riddle was a mortgage broker living in Highland Park. He loathed the long trip from his home to Midway. During the war, he'd been a navy transport pilot, so the solution was simple: he'd start a commuter airline from the North Shore to Midway.

Riddle used his business and flying contacts to gather a group of investors. The planned route was between Sky Harbor Airfield in Northbrook and Midway Airport. Early in 1951, the Civil Aeronautics Board gave its approval, and Riddle began buying equipment and hiring staff.

Midway Airlines began service on June 30, 1951. The Cessna single-engine plane took off from Midway at 2:00 p.m., landing at Sky Harbor twelve minutes later. All trips that day were made on schedule without incident. Trouble was—no passengers showed up.

But the following day, seventeen paying customers arrived. They came, they flew, and they were satisfied. From there, business grew slowly but steadily. By October, the industry journal *Flying* was able to pronounce the "world's shortest airline" a success.

Midway Airlines was soon flying fourteen regularly scheduled flights on the Sky Harbor–Midway run, between 6:00 a.m. and 11:00 p.m. daily. When traffic was heavy, a transport plane was pressed into service. The six-dollar one-way fare—about sixty-five dollars in today's money—was significantly cheaper than the average cab fare over the same route. And of course, the travel time was faster and the view was better.

But that was only the beginning. In 1952, the airline added flights between Chicago's downtown Meigs Field and Midway Airport. Service to DuPage County Airport followed. Reflecting its short-hop business model, Midway Airlines adopted a logo of a kangaroo carrying two suitcases hopping over a city skyline.

Publicity for Midway Airlines always noted that it was a full-fledged carrier, just like United, American, TWA, and the rest, operating from a regular Midway Airport terminal on a regular schedule. Tickets were sold by uniformed clerks, each flight had a uniformed stewardess, and every pilot had at least two thousand hours of flying time. Baggage up to forty pounds could be checked.

Still, the small size of the airline did present some homey touches. As a licensed pilot, President Hugh Riddle took his turn in the air and filled in wherever needed. On Christmas Day, when most of the staff was enjoying the holiday, he spent several hours plowing the airline's runway. One passenger recalled buying a ticket from Riddle, having Riddle collect the ticket at the gate, then flying off with Riddle piloting the plane.

By its fourth year in operation, Midway Airlines was carrying nearly two thousand passengers a month, with a perfect safety record. Still, there was at least one scary incident. A drunken man managed to get on a flight with his three children. Once in the air, he seemed to be making preparations to push them out the cabin door. With that, the pilot roared upward into a steep bank, throwing the man away from the door and knocking him out cold. The kids went on playing.

In 1955, O'Hare Airport opened northwest of the city. Though the new facility was still small, it offered travelers another alternative to Midway Airport. Business at Midway Airlines fell off sharply. The "Kangaroo Hop" airline made its final flights on March 4, 1956.

PESHTIGO COURT

Almost any Chicago street name tells a story. Take Peshtigo Court. Located at 500 east, it is the last street you cross on the way to Navy Pier, before you duck under the Lake Shore Drive viaduct. The one-block-long lane is named for a Wisconsin town north of Green Bay, about 250 miles from Chicago.

In 1871, Peshtigo was a booming lumber depot with a population of 1,700. Summer that year had been very hot—dry too, with total rainfall of less than two inches. Now, in the early days of October, many small fires were breaking out in the surrounding forest. Crews of volunteers had been kept busy extinguishing them.

October 8 was a Sunday. Just as Peshtigo was getting ready for bed, a heavy wind suddenly whipped in from the southwest. Then a wall of flame swept down on the town.

Within minutes, everything was burning. Men and women ran out of their homes in nightclothes. Peshtigo had no fire department, so residents gathered water in buckets to douse the flames. Soon they realized the fire was beyond their control. If they couldn't fight, flight was the answer. But where could they go?

The Peshtigo River seemed the safest place, and most people headed there. Others had different ideas. A couple of families took refuge in stone cellars. A few folks thought to jump down wells. That proved to be a mistake—as the fire came closer and heated the water in the wells, they were boiled alive. The temperature in the air pushed past one thousand degrees, about as hot as a crematorium. Just inhaling it caused instant death.

Meanwhile, chaos reigned at the river. The bridge had collapsed, cutting off escape from town. Burning debris rained down from the sky on the people huddled in the water. Some of them simply gave in to fatigue and sank below the surface. One man discovered that the burned woman he'd carried to safety was not his wife and became hysterical. A teenage girl stayed afloat by hanging onto the horn of a bull.

In little more than an hour, the flames moved on. Before it burned itself out the next day, the fire destroyed a dozen smaller villages and leveled an area as big as Rhode Island, taking an estimated 2,000 lives. Peshtigo alone lost 800 people. More than 350 victims were never identified and were buried in a mass grave.

Historians have advanced several theories about the origin of the Peshtigo fire. The consensus is that many small fires were whipped together by a

Peshtigo Court—a little street with a big story. *Photograph by the author.*

cyclonic wind into the one big blaze. Those smaller fires could have been caused by just about anything—embers from passing steam locomotives, slash-and-burn land clearance from farmers or loggers, campfires left carelessly untended, even shattered pieces from a falling meteor. The dry summer then provided the fuel to keep the super-fire burning.

The destruction of Peshtigo was a great tragedy. But what does an event in a little Wisconsin village have to do with Chicago history? And why do we have a central-area street named Peshtigo Court?

On the very same October 8, 1871, that Peshtigo was in flames—at the very same hour—the Great Chicago Fire was also burning. Over the course of two days, almost everything in the city east of the Chicago River, from Taylor Street north to Fullerton Avenue, was destroyed. The death toll was two hundred.

A major city had been leveled, and that was big news. Yet the Peshtigo fire was barely noted, even though ten times more people lost their lives. To the average American of 1871, backwoods Wisconsin was about as remote as Africa or India. Yeah, two thousand people died out there in the wilderness—too bad, let's move on.

Like Chicago, Peshtigo rebuilt. Today, the town is home to about 3,500 people. The local historical society maintains a fire museum, and various memorial events are held on or around October 8 each year.

Peshtigo remembers the victims of its 1871 fire. And in our own way, we in Chicago remember them, too.

CHICAGO DIBS

It happens every winter. A major snowfall hits Chicago. The next day, near the curbs on residential streets throughout the city, you'll find neatly shoveled spaces among the drifts. In the center of each space is a chair or a table or a crate or some other object. They spring up after every blizzard, like mushrooms after a thunderstorm.

If you're a Chicagoan, you'll understand. Someone has shoveled out that parking space and is reserving it for future use.

For many years, this local practice had no name—rolling out the old furniture to protect your parking space was just a natural reflex that didn't have to be justified or even named. Then some wiseacre began referring to it as "Dibs," using the term from our childhood games. That's what we call it today.

No one is sure when the custom originated. It may be as old as the Model T. My first memory of Dibs starts with the Blizzard of 1967.

A record twenty-three inches of snow in twenty-four hours fell on Chicago on January 26–27, 1967. Traffic became so snarled that first afternoon that thousands of motorists simply abandoned their cars and set off for home on foot. This was before snow routes. There was no real plan on what streets to clear first.

Within a few days of the first storm, the city was clobbered with fourteen inches more of snow. Then the weather turned frigid. The snow cover would last through St. Patrick's Day.

Meanwhile, out in the neighborhoods, Chicagoans began digging out their cars. After all that work, you weren't about to surrender your parking space, so you hauled out the furniture. If some clown violated protocol and invaded your territory, he risked retaliation involving broken antennas or flattened tires or worse.

A city street is a public thoroughfare. Everyday citizens don't have a right to save parking places. Still, in 1967 the city did not bother to enforce the

Chicago Dibs in action. *Photograph by the author.*

law. Perhaps Mayor Richard J. Daley reasoned that the shovelers had earned the right to their spaces. More likely, he didn't want to needlessly rile any voters. He was running for reelection in the spring.

So from 1967 on, Chicago Dibs has endured. A dozen years later, Mayor Michael Bilandic handled snow removal poorly after a blizzard and lost his own bid for reelection. Local politicians have learned that Chicagoans will get testy when the snow piles up. If that means letting a shoveler lay claim to a portion of a street, it is a small price to pay for staying in office.

In more recent times, reports have filtered in that Philadelphia, St. Louis, and other cities have copied the Dibs practice. However, though Chicago has made Dibs famous, we may not have invented it.

We are told that people in Pittsburgh have been saving shoveled-out parking spots for decades—and if you've ever driven on the narrow streets on some of their hills, you'll understand why. Some sources even refer to a piece of furniture planted in a cleared space as a Pittsburgh Chair. There are said to be photos showing Pittsburgh Dibs back in the 1950s. Still, Stefan Lorant's massive pictorial *Pittsburgh: The Story of an American City* doesn't have anything about it. Maybe Pittsburgh Dibs wasn't a citywide practice but only a few isolated incidents.

Whether Chicago Dibs will endure is an open question. A younger generation, with no memory of the grim blizzards of the past, seems ready to abandon the tradition. Already a few neighborhoods have posted signs announcing, "This Is a Chair-Free Zone." City officials have warned that they will no longer tolerate the unlawful saving of parking spaces. Maybe they really mean business and will clear out all the chairs and tables and lamps and religious statues.

And once the crews have collected all that furniture, what are they going to do with it? Can the owners retrieve a confiscated chair by paying a fine, like you do when your car is towed? Or will the city have a giant flea market sale in the spring? Chicago Dibs may prove to be an even greater source of revenue than speed cameras.

ABOUT THE AUTHOR

John R. Schmidt is a fifth-generation Chicagoan. He earned his AB and MA degrees at Loyola University and his PhD in history at the University of Chicago. He has taught at all levels, from kindergarten through college, including over thirty years in the Chicago Public School system. He has published over five hundred articles in magazines, newspapers, encyclopedias, and anthologies. This is his seventh book.

Visit us at
www.historypress.com